✳

Crime and the American Dream

Bernard Henry Levy (i)

Crime and the American Dream

FOURTH EDITION

STEVEN F. MESSNER
University at Albany
State University of New York

RICHARD ROSENFELD
University of Missouri–St. Louis

Australia • Brazil • Canada • Mexico • Singapore • Spain
United Kingdom • United States

THOMSON
™
WADSWORTH

Crime and the American Dream,
Fourth Edition
Steven F. Messner and Richard Rosenfeld

Vice President, Editor-in-Chief: Eve Howard
Acquisition Editor: Carolyn Henderson Meier
Assistant Editor: Jana Davis
Editorial Assistant: Rebecca Johnson
Technology Project Manager: Susan De Vanna
Marketing Manager: Terra Schultz
Marketing Assistant: Jaren Boland
Marketing Communication Manager: Linda Yip
Project Manager, Editorial Production: Matt Ballantyne
Creative Director: Rob Hugel

Print Buyer: Linda Hsu
Permissions Editor: Kiely Sisk
Production Service: Aaron Downey, Matrix
    Productions Inc.
Copy Editor: Cheryl Smith
Cover Designer: Yvo Riezbos
Cover Image: Copyright © Christopher
    Zacharow/Images.com
Compositor: Integra
Text and Cover Printer: Webcom, Limited

Thomson Higher Education
10 Davis Drive
Belmont, CA 94002-3098
USA

For more information about our products,
contact us at:
Thomson Learning Academic Resource Center
1-800-423-0563

For permission to use material from this text or
product, submit a request online at
http://www.thomsonrights.com.
Any additional questions about permissions can be
submitted by e-mail to
thomsonrights@thomson.com.

Nothing happens unless first a dream.
—Carl Sandburg

Contents

Preface

This book has been written with two purposes in mind: first, to present a plausible explanation of the exceptionally high levels of serious crime in the United States; second, to formulate this explanation using the basic ideas, insights, and conceptual tools of sociology.

Each of these purposes rests on an underlying premise, one empirical, and the other epistemological. The empirical premise views crime rates as in fact exceptionally high in the United States. While some level of criminal activity may be a normal feature of all societies, as Émile Durkheim proposed almost a century ago, both the level of and the preoccupation with serious crime in America are quite striking, especially when comparing the United States with other highly developed nations. We report both quantitative and qualitative evidence in the book to support our empirical claim about the distinctiveness of the American experience with crime.

An important epistemological premise also informs our inquiry. We are convinced that the formulation of a satisfactory explanation of cross-national variation in crime will require the systematic application of sociological knowledge and principles, which together comprise the "sociological perspective." Some sociologists will undoubtedly reject the notion that there is any common intellectual terrain that can be so described. Nonetheless, although we recognize the intellectual diversity in the field, we remain convinced that a set of common concepts and assumptions forms the corpus of the discipline. This is, after all, what we teach our students year after year and what we require as part of a core curriculum for both graduate and undergraduate students. In a sense, then, we set out in this book to "put sociology to work" on a substantive problem of considerable theoretical and practical significance. The great advantage of the sociological perspective, in our view, is that it requires that attention be paid to both of the fundamental features of any organized social system: people's beliefs, values, goals—the stuff of culture—and the positions and roles that people occupy in society—what sociologists term "social structure." Neither of these

ix

two basic features of social organization may be ignored *a priori* in sociological analysis. It may, of course, turn out that a particular social phenomenon, such as crime, is more heavily dependent on one or the other of these features. But this must be demonstrated; it cannot be assumed. The sociological burden of proof always rests with those who would cast out one of the basic aspects of social organization and privilege the other. The focus on both culture and social structure, and on the interplay between them, has been an invaluable analytical tool for evaluating the strengths and weaknesses of influential explanations of crime, as well as for developing our own thesis.

Even though the sociological perspective underlies our explanation of crime, we wrote *Crime and the American Dream* hoping that it would be used in a variety of disciplines and courses. Within sociology, it is suitable for the introductory course and courses on social problems, American society, criminology, and sociological theory. In criminology and criminal justice, it fits well in the introductory course and could be used in specialized courses on violent crime, comparative criminology, and theories of crime. In fact, the book has been adopted in these courses and more, at both upper and lower levels. It also has been used in graduate courses on violent crime and criminological theory.

We also intended to say something meaningful to our professional colleagues about the interconnections of crime and social organization, and we have been heartened by the critical response to our ideas in the scholarly literature. Finally, we wrote with a broader readership in mind. Anyone curious about the way American society "ticks" and how crime reveals both the best and the worst of the American experience should find the argument in *Crime and the American Dream* of interest.

THE ARGUMENT

The essence of our argument is that the distinctive patterns and levels of crime in the United States are produced by the cultural and structural organization of American society. A strong emphasis on the goal of monetary success and a weak emphasis on the importance of the legitimate means for the pursuit of success characterize American culture. This combination of strong pressures to succeed monetarily and weak restraints on the selection of means is intrinsic to the dominant cultural ethos: the American Dream. The "American Dream" refers to a cultural commitment to the goal of economic success, to be pursued by everyone under conditions of open, individual competition. The American Dream contributes to crime directly by encouraging people to employ illegal means to achieve goals that are culturally approved. It also exerts an indirect effect on crime through its interconnections with the institutional balance of power in society.

The American Dream promotes and sustains an institutional structure in which one institution—the economy—assumes dominance over all others. The resulting imbalance in the institutional structure diminishes the capacity of other institutions, such as the family, education, and the political system, to curb crime-fostering cultural pressures and to impose controls over and provide support for the members of society. In these ways, the distinctive cultural commitments of the American Dream and its companion institutional arrangements contribute to high levels of crime.

Although we began writing this book convinced of the general thesis that high levels of crime in the United States are related to basic features of social organization, we never anticipated many of the specific arguments that have emerged as a result of our intellectual efforts. Novelists and playwrights describe how characters and plot can assume "a life of their own" and lead the author in unforeseen directions. Something like this occurred as we worked our way through the connections between crime and the American Dream. The use of the sociological perspective necessitated a more systematic and critical appraisal of existing theory and research on crime—including our own—than we intended.

At the beginning, we conceived of this book as a summary statement of criminological research within the "anomie" tradition, where much of our research has been located, and as a call for continued work in this area. However, the sociological perspective led us to rethink some of the basic assumptions and interpretations of anomie theory, such as the presumed association between crime and social inequality. We continue to believe that anomie theory offers significant insights regarding the nature of crime and of the American crime problem in particular. But the contributions of anomie theory, and those of alternative theoretical approaches, will be realized fully only when situated in a more general sociological perspective on crime and social organization.

Writing this book was a process of discovery or, more precisely, rediscovery of the value of the sociological way of viewing the world. Although we have developed an explanation of crime that differs from other explanations in important respects, many of the ideas underlying our explanation are not original; they are part of the common heritage of modern sociology. Our thinking about culture, social structure, and crime fits within an intellectual environment shaped by Émile Durkheim, Alexis de Tocqueville, and Karl Marx. Our analysis of social institutions is highly compatible with the important contribution of Robert Bellah and his colleagues in *The Good Society*. Our conception of sociological inquiry has been influenced by scholars as diverse as Talcott Parsons and C. Wright Mills, both of whom insisted that the separate parts of a society always must be understood with reference to the whole. Finally, we owe an incalculable intellectual debt to Robert K. Merton, on whose shoulders our sociological explanation of crime stands most directly.

THE PLAN OF THE BOOK

Chapter 1 introduces the central premise of our explanation of crime, namely, that high levels of serious crime result from the normal functioning of the American social system. This chapter also presents the core components of the

American Dream. We describe how they contribute to the openness and dynamic quality of American society, as well as to "the dark side" of the American experience: high rates of crime. Chapter 1 ends with a description of Merton's formulation of the anomie perspective on crime. We suggest that, despite ups and downs over time in the appeal of Merton's argument to criminologists, and significant substantive limitations that are addressed in subsequent chapters, anomie theory has enduring value in the study of crime.

In Chapter 2, we describe in detail the nature of the crime problem in the contemporary United States. We present evidence on "crimes in the streets," "crimes in the suites," and the extraordinary levels of incarceration to substantiate the underlying empirical premise of the book, that there is indeed something distinctive about crime and the response to crime in the United States. The descriptive material in Chapter 2 essentially reveals, in the form of statistical indicators and human responses, a social reality of crime that a comprehensive sociological theory must be capable of explaining.

We turn in Chapter 3 to a review of the dominant sociological perspectives in contemporary criminology. We consider the more individualistic, social-psychological approaches to crime as well as their macrolevel analogues. Each of the perspectives reviewed contains valuable insights about the origins of crime, but each is also limited in important respects. We propose that, among conventional approaches, the anomie perspective holds the greatest promise for a macrolevel explanation of crime because it incorporates into its explanatory framework both cultural and structural dynamics. We also identify the more important limitations of conventional anomie theory, especially the curious neglect by supporters and critics alike of social institutions.

Chapter 4 presents our macrosociological explanation of crime. We identify the anomic tendencies of the American Dream—the penchant to pursue goals by "any means necessary"—and show how these tendencies are both reflected in and reproduced by an institutional structure dominated by the economy. Our analysis focuses on four major social institutions: the family, the educational system, the political system, and, of course, the economy. We substantiate our claim of institutional imbalance by pointing to three manifestations of economic dominance: (1) the *devaluation* of noneconomic functions and roles, (2) the *accommodation* to economic demands required of other institutions, and (3) the *penetration* into other institutional domains of economic standards. Finally, we discuss how high levels of serious crime are produced by the combination of anomic cultural orientations and weak noneconomic institutions.

We conclude in Chapter 5 with an extended discussion of the theoretical and policy implications of the analysis. Our thesis offers a serious challenge to both criminological theorists and policy makers. It implies that criminological theories that neglect the ironic interdependence between crime and the normal functioning of the social system will be unable to explain the American experience with crime. Moreover, if our analysis is valid, significant reductions in crime will not result from conservative "get tough" policies of crime control, nor from conventional liberal proposals to broaden access to the American Dream. Effective crime control will, instead, require fundamental transformations in the organization of American society and a rethinking of a dream that is the envy of the world.

THE FOURTH EDITION

Just over a decade has passed since the publication of the first edition of *Crime and the American Dream*. Changes having a direct bearing on our central thesis have occurred in crime and punishment since the early 1990s. The revisions to the fourth edition reflect our efforts to confront the intellectual challenges posed by some of those changes.

As with previous editions, we have thoroughly updated statistics, added relevant citations to the recent scholarly literature, incorporated new illustrations, and pruned dated materials. Discussions of the Enron corporate scandal and the terrorist attacks of September 11, 2001, have been added for purposes of setting up the arguments in Chapters 1 and 2 respectively. In Chapter 4, we have slightly revised the diagram of the analytic model of the linkages between macrosocial organization and crime to highlight the consequences of economic dominance for institutional *support*. We concur with Cullen and Wright's view that a full sociological explanation of crime requires attention not only to the control function of social institutions but also to their capacity to provide social support.[1] Chapter 5 introduces a new discussion of sentencing reform and issues surrounding prisoner reentry to reflect current policy challenges and debates within the field. The main point of this section remains the same. In our view, setting limits on the reach of correctional control is a promising strategy for reducing levels of crime in the long run.

Perhaps the most important revision in the current edition relates to the premise of "American exceptionalism" in crime. We have had to reconsider this premise in view of the noteworthy convergence in crime rates between the United States and other developed nations. When we wrote the first edition, American violent crime rates were escalating, and the United States held a commanding lead over other developed nations in rates of serious violent crime, robbery and homicide in particular. A decade of falling violent crime rates in the United States and rises in many other developed nations led us to pay greater attention in this edition to cross-national differences in the *social response* to crime. American incarceration rates have risen dramatically, and the United States holds a greater fraction of its population in prisons and jails than any other nation in the world.[2] In its punishment policies, American society is more exceptional than ever. Changes in the scale of incarceration, we have concluded, must be incorporated in any meaningful comparison of U.S. crime rates with those of other nations.

Our effort to formulate an integrated explanation of the distinctiveness of crime and punishment in the United States is indebted to Elliott Currie's cogent analysis of the ways in which incarceration may suppress crime while hiding socially generated "criminality."[3] Part of the reason for the recent convergence across nations in violent crime rates is that the United States has embarked on an unprecedented social experiment: the mass incapacitation of criminal offenders through secure confinement. Mass incarceration has probably suppressed official crime rates, making them closer to those elsewhere. But has mass incarceration reduced the level of *criminality*—the motivation to engage in criminal behavior—or has it merely reduced the opportunity to commit crimes through the quarantining of criminal offenders in prisons and jails? We raise this provocative question in the revised section on the social response to crime in Chapter 2, and in Chapter 5 we discuss several policies directed at reducing both criminality *and* incarceration.

The concluding sentence of the preface to the third edition stated our hope that the thesis developed in *Crime and the American Dream* would remain alive in the discipline and in public discourse. This hope once again motivates the writing of another edition and, as in the past, we eagerly await our readers' lively, constructive, and critical responses to our arguments, both old and new.

Richard Rosenfeld
Steven F. Messner

October 2005

ACKNOWLEDGMENTS

We are grateful to those colleagues who have taken the time to write to us about their own and their students' reactions to *Crime and the American Dream*, as well as to the reviewers who have offered such competent criticism and guidance over multiple editions of the book. The latter include Robert Agnew, Emory University; William R. Arnold, University of Kansas; Thomas J. Bernard, Pennsylvania State University; David Bordua, University of Illinois; Robert J. Bursik, Jr., University of Illinois-St. Louis; Mitchell B. Chamlin, University of Cincinnati; Roland Chilton, University of Massachusetts at Amherst; Richard Hawkins, Southern Methodist State University; Nella Lee, Portland State University; Robert F. Meier, Iowa State University; Gary Rabe, Minot State University; John Stratton, University of Iowa; and Austin Turk, University of California, Riverside. Richard Wright of the University of Missouri–St. Louis provided constructive and helpful comments on various aspects of our argument. Michael Ostrowsky, University at Albany, SUNY, provided valuable assistance with the updating of statistics. Serina Beauparlant, our original editor at Wadsworth, enthusiastically supported the book from the outset. Her encouragement bolstered our confidence on more than one occasion when we began to doubt the merits of the project. We are grateful to Sabra Horne for initiating the current edition and to Carolyn Henderson Meier for seeing it through the production process.

This book is dedicated to our families, who have facilitated and tempered our pursuit of the American Dream.

NOTES

1. Cullen and Wright (1997).
2. Mauer (2003).
3. Currie (1999).

1

A Society Organized for Crime

Winning isn't everything; it's the only thing.
VINCE LOMBARDI,
(FOOTBALL COACH)

By any means necessary.
MALCOLM X,
(BLACK NATIONALIST)

At the beginning of the 21st century, Enron was the seventh largest corporation in the United States and was poised, in the words of former chairman Kenneth Lay, to become "the world's leading company." Within a year, its stock lost 90 percent of its value, Moody's Investor's Services downgraded its debt to "junk" status, and Enron filed for bankruptcy. Federal prosecutors began filing charges against corporate officers for crimes including money laundering, obstruction of justice, and securities and wire fraud. Most of the criminal charges were connected to Enron's alleged concealment of massive losses in a vast network of interlocking limited partnerships, thereby maintaining the appearance of profitability and artificially inflating stock prices. When signs of its impending collapse began to emerge, Enron officials prohibited employees from withdrawing their savings from the company's pension plan. Meanwhile, many of those same officials dumped their stock holdings and earned huge profits just before Enron's financial difficulties were made public. Employees and other shareholders lost an estimated $63 billion after Enron filed for bankruptcy in December 2001. Most of the employees lost more than 90 percent of their retirement funds. As one account phrased it, their "American Dream" had "become a national nightmare."[1]

As of summer 2004, 31 people had been charged in connection with the federal investigation of Enron, including founder and chairman Kenneth Lay, who was indicted on 11 counts of conspiracy, fraud, and making false statements to banks.[2] Former CEO Jeffrey Skilling was indicted on charges including 42 counts of wire fraud, securities fraud, insider trading, and other felonies. A brilliant, aggressive, larger-than-life figure, Skilling was known at Enron for his disdain for convention "be it with office furniture and dress codes or the rules about how companies should grow or control their workers. Creativity was his guiding principle, caution was anathema." He was more concerned with results, the bottom line, than with the methods used to get there. He helped to shape a highly competitive "growth-at-any-cost" corporate culture that rewarded, seemingly above all else, short-run profitability, or at least the appearance of it, and a corresponding impatience with "rules."[3]

The name "Enron" became synonymous with a rash of scandals that hit other corporate giants during the first years of the 21st century.[4] But corporate scandals are nothing new in America. More than a decade before the Enron scandal, the nation was shocked by the wheeling and dealing of the Wall Street traders of so-called junk bonds. The term "junk bond" was coined to refer to high-risk, high-yield bonds that were often used to facilitate swift corporate buyouts and takeovers. Trading in junk bonds could be extraordinarily lucrative, especially for those willing to ignore the "technicalities" of the federal securities laws.

One of the most notorious and controversial of the junk-bond traders was Michael Milken. Milken headed the high-yield bond department of Drexel Burnham Lambert during the 1980s, a time of soaring profits for many Wall Street traders. Milken himself made out handsomely. According to government estimates, he earned approximately $296 million in 1986 and $550 million in 1987.[5] Milken paid a price, however, for his success. A significant share of his lucrative earnings derived from insider trading and other illegal activities. He was eventually convicted of violating federal securities laws and, in November 1990, he was sentenced to 10 years in prison, a three-year term of probation, and 5400 hours of community service. His prison sentence was reduced to two years in return for his cooperation in subsequent investigations.[6]

Milken's misdeeds elicited an ambivalent reaction from the general public. On the one hand, he was chastised for taking advantage of his powerful position. A *New York Times* editorial applauded the stiff penalty handed down to Milken, observing that the court had sent a "wake-up call" to the financial community, signaling the end of lenient punishments for crimes on Wall Street.[7] On the other hand, while critics viewed the junk bond as a destructive weapon of corporate warfare, Milken and his supporters saw his activities as creative financial innovations that would help reform the American economy. He had, after all, used junk bonds to provide much needed credit for hundreds of new companies.

Upon his release from prison, Milken was invited to teach occasional courses at UCLA's graduate business school. The idea of a convicted white-collar criminal teaching business students elicited the same contradictory reactions that accompanied his earlier conviction and sentencing. A UCLA science student remarked, "I resent Milken's being here. . . . This is an institution of higher education, not a place for opportunists to make money." In contrast, another student described Milken as "a great man—a martyr, not a crook." Both students seem to be responding to many of the same qualities in Milken, especially what one journalist has called his "bottom-line fanaticism" and innovative spirit.[8]

Such cases of financial misdeeds illustrate the paradoxes inherent in the sources of and responses to crime in the United States. The very qualities in which Michael Milken took pride and for which he was praised—his daring, energy, intelligence, and, most important, his ability to create and willingness to use innovative solutions for conventional problems—also led to his crimes and punishment. Enron's Jeffrey Skilling was similarly described as "brilliant, innovative, visionary, and driven."[9] These are elements of social character rooted in broad value orientations within American culture that help shape both the archetypal American hero and the archetypal American villain. An even more fundamental sociological principle is revealed by Milken, Skilling, and the culture at Enron: the ironic interdependence between good and evil in social life. As the sociologist Kai Erikson explains, "The deviant and the conformist . . . are creatures of the same culture, inventions of the same imagination."[10] To understand fully the nature and level of crime in a society, therefore, it is essential to consider the distinguishing features of that society, particularly its distinctive cultural imagination.

CRIME AND RESPONSES TO CRIME IN AMERICA

The ironic interdependence of deviance and conformity applies not only to the kinds of financial crimes that occur with alarming regularity in the United States but to crime more generally, including crimes of violence. Indeed, although property crimes and violent crimes might appear on the surface to be quite different, many violent street crimes are similar in an important respect to the "suite" crimes of high finance. They involve a willingness to innovate, that is, to use technically efficient but illegitimate means to solve conventional problems.

The Nature and Level of Criminal Violence

Fictional accounts of violent crime frequently involve exotic motives and elaborate planning. In fact, most criminal violence is quite mundane—the outcome of a commonplace dispute between a victim and an offender who know one another. These disputes often arise from economic transactions gone awry. The following two scenarios, drawn from police case files in St. Louis, illustrate the role of homicide in settling disputes related to drug transactions:

> Suspect bought two bags of coke from victim. One of the bags was not dope. Suspect followed victim and witness in a car. Victim stopped his car, got out, and began approaching suspect's car. Suspect opened fire. Victim dead on scene.

> Victim was a "runner"—delivering drugs for a seller. He was nervous because he was short his "turn in." A friend lent him $2,500 cash the evening before the victim was killed. Victim liked to "flash" cash and expensive jewelry, and talk about what he could afford to buy. The seller denied having anything to do with victim's death. He was later murdered.

A common theme of an economic dispute that is settled by the use of violent means runs through these events. The disputes arise from economic problems that are quite conventional in origin (faulty or fraudulent merchandise, payments overdue, bad debts). However, none of these problems or the resulting disputes can be settled through conventional (that is, legal) means, because they all involve illegal activities. With access to conventional dispute-resolution mechanisms (lawyers, courts, legally imposed restitution, fines, and so forth) blocked in these cases, their resolution requires the innovative use of unconventional means. Many crimes, including homicides, have been characterized as a form of "self-help" directed at rule infractions for which conventional legal responses are either ineffective or, as in these cases, unavailable.[11]

The use of violent means to achieve or regain control in underworld markets, like the use of illegal nonviolent means (such as price fixing or insider trading) to control legitimate markets, receives strong, if indirect, cultural support in our society. High rates of gun-related violence, in particular, result in part from a cultural ethos that encourages the rapid deployment of technically efficient methods to solve interpersonal problems. The widespread availability of firearms, and their use by offenders and rule enforcers alike, represent not simply the strength or persistence of a "gun culture," which itself requires explanation, but a much deeper cultural orientation that permits or does not strongly discourage the attainment of goals "by any means necessary."

This "anything goes" mentality results in a U.S. volume of criminal violence, and lethal violence in particular, that is truly remarkable in comparative context. Despite significant declines during the 1990s (discussed in the next chapter), the U.S. homicide rate remains higher than that of all other advanced nations in the world. In 2000, more homicides occurred in Washington, DC, than in Amsterdam, Berlin, Paris, and Rome *combined*.[12]

Fear of Crime

Not surprisingly, high levels of violent crime in the United States result in widespread fear of crime. One-third of the adult population—and 44 percent of black American adults—fears walking alone at night in their own neighborhoods.[13] In the inner cities, parents sometimes feel compelled to keep their children inside—a confinement that young people in the 1990s began referring to as "lockdown," an ironic term borrowed from the lexicon of prison life.[14] Fear of crime has been shown to reduce residents' satisfaction with their neighborhoods and to instill a desire to abandon the neighborhood for safer surroundings. One observer suggested that fear of crime, more than racial prejudice, was responsible for the spring 1992 acquittal of four white police officers in the widely publicized beating in Los Angeles of Rodney King, a black man. That verdict sparked some of the most serious urban rioting in recent U.S. history.[15]

The pervasive fear of crime observed in the United States is not an inevitable feature of advanced industrial societies. On the contrary, it is a distinctly American phenomenon. Freda Adler, a comparative criminologist who has studied crime in many nations throughout the modern world, concludes that the American

> preoccupation with crime is not a national past-time in more countries than one. Neither the design of doors and windows, nor the front page stories in the national press, nor the budgetary allocations of municipal and national governments indicate any obsession with crime, the fear of crime, the fear of victimization, or indeed, the national destiny.[16]

Crime Control

Like high levels of crime and fear of crime, punitive means of social control are taken-for-granted facts of life in the United States. The United States has the highest incarceration rate in the world. As of the end of 2002, more than two million Americans were serving time in a prison or local jail, a rate of 701 inmates per 100,000 residents.[17]

Levels of incarceration for selected subpopulations in the United States, particularly for socially disadvantaged groups, are even more astonishing. Ten percent of black men age 25 to 29 resided in a state or federal prison in 2002, compared to 2 percent of Hispanic men and 1 percent of white men of the same age. Yet, in spite of record levels of incarceration and expansions in other forms of correctional control, 88 percent of Americans believe that the courts are too lenient with criminals.[18] Even though the United States locks up a greater proportion of its residents than any other nation on Earth—and thereby manages to obscure part of its crime problem—most Americans believe the criminal justice system is too easy on lawbreakers. In short, like crime itself, crime control in the United States is driven by a strong, at times desperate, emphasis on ends over means.

How can we explain the facts of crime and punishment that distinguish the United States from nearly all other developed nations? Has something "gone wrong" in America that accounts for high levels of crime, fear, and punitive sanctions? Or, on the contrary, is there something about the very nature of American society that generates distinctive forms and levels of crime that remain remarkably resistant to social reform and social control?

Our answer, hinted at in the previous discussion, can be stated quite simply, but with far-reaching implications: High crime rates are intrinsic to the basic cultural commitments and institutional arrangements of American society. In short, at all social levels, America is organized for crime.

THE VIRTUES AND VICES OF THE AMERICAN DREAM

In this book, we locate the sources of crime in the very same values and behaviors that are conventionally viewed as part of the American success story. From this vantage point, high rates of crime in the United States do not arise from the "sick" outcome of individual pathologies, such as defective personalities or aberrant biological structures. Neither are they the "evil" consequence of individual moral failings, such as greed.[19] Nor does the American crime problem simply reflect universally condemned social conditions, such as poverty and discrimination, or ineffective law enforcement, or lax punishment of criminals. Rather, crime in America derives, in significant measure, from highly prized cultural and social conditions.

This book proposes that the American Dream itself and the normal social conditions engendered by it are deeply implicated in the problem of crime. In our use of the term "the American Dream," we refer to a broad cultural ethos that entails a commitment to the goal of material success, to be pursued by everyone in society, under conditions of open, individual competition. The American Dream has both an evaluative and a cognitive dimension associated with it. People are socialized to accept the desirability of pursuing the goal of material success, and they are encouraged to believe that the chances of realizing the Dream are sufficiently high to justify a continued commitment to this cultural goal. These beliefs and commitments in many respects define what it means to be an enculturated member of our society. The ethos refers quite literally to the *American* dream.

Evolution of the Concept of the American Dream

The term "the American Dream" was introduced into contemporary social analysis in 1931 by historian James Truslow Adams to describe his vision of a society open to individual achievement. Interestingly, Adams fought to have his history of the United States, *Epic of America*, entitled *The American Dream*, but his publisher rejected the idea, believing that during the Great Depression, consumers would never spend three dollars "on a dream."[20] The publisher clearly misread the popular mood, because the general public proved to be highly receptive to the notion of the American Dream. The term soon became a sales slogan for the material comforts and individual opportunities of a middle-class lifestyle: a car, a house, education for the children, a secure retirement.

Cultural histories of the general "success" theme in literature testify to the remarkable durability of the American Dream over the course of the past century. For example, research by Charles Hearn documents the persistence of the American Dream in the popular imagination despite the profound social changes ushered in by the Great Depression. Hearn systematically reviews a wide range of literary sources published during the 1920s and 1930s, including manuals, guidebooks, and inspirational works on success, popular magazine biographies and fiction, and the fiction of highly regarded "serious" writers. He discovers that the Great Depression altered the American Dream in subtle ways, making it more "complex, confusing, and contradictory."[21] At the same time, however, Hearn concludes that the American Dream per se was not rejected, nor was it replaced. It endured, Hearn speculates, because "the myth of success has penetrated American culture much too completely for a single crisis, even one as harrowing as the Great Depression, to deal it the death blow."[22]

Elizabeth Long, who has analyzed cultural changes in the United States during the years following World War II, documents the persistence of the American Dream. Long examines the shifting meanings of the dream of success as reflected in best-selling novels published between 1945 and 1975. Like Hearn, Long identifies some important changes in the collective vision of success that have occurred in response to various historical circumstances. She notes, in particular, a weakening of the commitment to an "entrepreneurial ethos"—that is, an ethos according to which the pursuit of individual self-interest necessarily promotes social progress. Significantly, her study does not extend to the "Reagan revolution" of the 1980s and the consolidation of the conservative agenda beginning in the 1990s, which rehabilitated the idea that the self-interested pursuit of economic success promotes the common good. In any event, Long emphasizes that the core components of the American Dream were reflected in popular writing throughout the 30-year period following World War II, and she concludes that no new cultural ethos has emerged to replace the traditional view of success.[23]

The extent to which this term continues to permeate discourse about success in the contemporary literature reflects the salience of the American Dream in the public consciousness. A Google computer search of the keywords *American* and *Dream* at the time of this writing produced over 4.7 million returns. The links cover topics as diverse as the American Dream in conjunction with immigrants, love, real estate, LSD, suburban sprawl, needlework, recreational vehicles, focus groups, cyberspace, buying, selling, borrowing, lending, and leasing. In short, today as in the past, the dream of individual material success continues to captivate the popular imagination in the United States, serving as a cultural compass guiding Americans in their everyday lives.

The Dark Side of the American Dream

The strong and persistent appeal of the American Dream has without question been highly beneficial for our society. The commitments associated with this cultural ethos have provided the motivational dynamic for economic expansion, extraordinary technological innovation, and high rates of social mobility. But there is a paradoxical quality to the American Dream. The very features that are responsible for the impressive accomplishments of American society have less desirable consequences as well. The American Dream is a mixed blessing, contributing to both the best and the worst elements of the American character and society. In the words of sociologist Robert K. Merton, "A cardinal American virtue, 'ambition,' promotes a cardinal American vice, 'deviant behavior.'"[24]

The cultural emphasis on achievement, which promotes productivity and innovation, also generates pressures to succeed at any cost. The glorification of individual competition, which fosters ambition and mobility, drives people apart and weakens the sense of community. Finally, the preoccupation with monetary rewards, which undergirds economic demand in a market economy, severely restricts the kinds of achievements to which people are motivated to aspire.

Monetary Success and Noneconomic Roles   The exaggerated priority given to *monetary* rewards has particularly important ramifications for the cultural valuation placed on roles performed in noneconomic contexts. Tasks that are primarily noneconomic in nature tend to receive meager cultural support, and the skillful performance of these tasks elicits little public recognition. Consider the meaning of education in America. A "good" education has historically been part of the middle-class success package. However, education has been viewed primarily as a means to an end. The portrait of the American Dream neglects the image of "a good student" as an intrinsically worthy ideal. Nor do Americans accord much respect to teachers, as reflected in the old adage "Those who can, do; those who can't, teach."[25]

Similar dynamics can be observed within the realm of the family. A "devoted parent" occupies a rather tenuous position in the American Dream. This devotion commonly relates to measures of the capacity to provide "a better life" or "a chance to get ahead"—that is, opportunities for economic success—for one's children. To this end, a rising fraction of the mothers of even very young children reenter or never leave the paid labor force. In 2001, 62 percent of married women with children under the age of 6 worked outside the home full- or part-time. This has greatly increased demand for child-care services and facilities in the United States. By the turn of the 21st century, only 23 percent of pre-kindergarten children between the ages of 3 and 5 were cared for by their parents alone. Fully 59 percent were enrolled in a daycare center, and the remainder were cared for by relatives or through other arrangements. The escalating costs of such care for young children impose a heavy financial burden both on state budgets and on low-income families who rely on government assistance to meet childcare and other expenses. State and federal childcare assistance has not kept pace. In the words of a 2003 report issued by the Children's Defense Fund on cuts in child-care assistance, reductions in government spending mean "that countless families will be worrying about the basic health and safety of their children."[26] In sum, the lack of emphasis on *parenting* in the American Dream has contributed to the outsourcing of childcare as parents try to balance the competing demands of work and family.

Also relevant for our purposes, the American Dream lacks a concern with citizenship and the performance of political roles for the furtherance of the collective good. The culture emphasizes individual success, and the role of government is viewed with considerable suspicion and is conceived of largely in terms of its capacity to facilitate individual material advancement, such as by lowering taxes. In short, the materialistic element of the American Dream emphasizes achievements in one exclusive domain of social life and implicitly devalues achievements and performances in all others. In so doing, the American Dream generates exceptionally strong pressures to succeed in a narrowly defined way and to pursue such success by the technically most efficient means, that is, by any means necessary.

Universalism and Economic Inequality   Another feature of the American Dream that has paradoxical implications is its *universalism*. All Americans, regardless of social origins or social location, are encouraged to embrace the tenets of the dominant cultural ethos. The imperative to succeed, or at least to keep on trying to succeed, respects no social boundaries. This universalism of goals is in many respects a matter of pride for Americans. It reflects an underlying democratic ethos and a belief in a common entitlement for everyone in society. Yet this universal application of the goal of monetary success inevitably creates serious dilemmas for large numbers of individuals in a social structure characterized by appreciable economic inequality. Because the culture precludes the possibility of noncompeting groups, and because it assigns higher priority to monetary success than to other goals, the status of being economically "unequal" is readily equated with being "unsuccessful" and, by extension, "unworthy."

It might thus seem reasonable to expect that the universalism inherent in the American Dream naturally tends to produce an egalitarian social structure. Accordingly, the current level of inequality in the United States might be viewed as something of an aberration, a temporary mismatch between culture and social structure—a betrayal of the American Dream.[27] At first glance, evidence seems to support such a position. Economic inequalities have in fact grown in recent years. For example, the share of income received by the poorest fifth of American families dropped from 5.3 percent in 1980 to 4.2 percent in 2001. The share received by the richest fifth increased from 41.1 percent to 47.7 percent over the same period. And income became even more concentrated *within* the top fifth of families. The percentage of income going to the richest 5 percent of families rose from 14.6 percent in 1980 to 21.0 percent in 2001.[28]

However, recent changes in economic inequality should not obscure the more fundamental *stability* that has characterized the basic contours of the distribution of income and wealth in the United States over time. The poorest fifth of families and unattached individuals have consistently received between 4 and 6 percent, and the richest fifth, between 40 and 50 percent, of total income throughout the period extending from the end of World War II to the present. As one economist has noted, while the distribution of family income has exhibited "drifts" toward slightly lower and higher levels of inequality over these decades, the changes have been modest.[29]

The distribution of wealth is even more concentrated than the distribution of income, and it also shows striking historical stability. The available data are rough, but it appears that the richest 1 percent of the U.S. population has owned somewhere between 20 and over 30 percent of all assets in America since the 1820s. Recent estimates from the Federal Reserve are at the high end of this range, with the richest 1 percent of all families holding 34 percent of total household net worth in 2001.[30] In other words, despite dramatic social changes over time — massive shifts in the occupational structure, the movement of the population from farm to city to suburb, booms and busts in the business cycle, transitions back and forth from Republican to Democratic administrations, and a host of governmental interventions and regulations — the American economic structure has been characterized consistently by substantial economic inequality.

We suggest that the best understanding of the pronounced and persistent economic inequality in the United States comes not as a departure from fundamental cultural orientations but rather as an expression of them. Despite the universalistic component of the American Dream, the basic logic of this cultural ethos actually *presupposes* high levels of inequality. A competitive allocation of monetary rewards requires both winners and losers, and winning and losing have meaning only when rewards are distributed unequally. The motivation to endure the competitive struggle is not maintained easily if the monetary difference between winning and losing is inconsequential. In short, the very fabric of the American Dream weaves a fundamental tension. It provides the cultural foundation for a high level of economic inequality, yet a high level of inequality relegates large segments of the population to the role of "failure" as defined by the standards of the very same cultural ethos.

The American Dream thus has a dark side that must be considered in any serious effort to uncover the social sources of crime. It encourages an exaggerated emphasis on monetary achievements while devaluing alternative criteria of success; it promotes a preoccupation with the realization of goals while de-emphasizing the importance of the ways in which the goals are pursued; and it helps create and sustain social structures incapable of restraining criminogenic cultural pressures.

The general idea that many of the same features of American society that contribute to its successes also produce crime is not new. This notion, which can be termed the "criminogenic hypothesis," was part of the critical social problems literature that flourished in the United States during the 1960s. A good example of this social criticism is Edwin Schur's provocative *Our Criminal Society,* published in 1969.[31] However, as shown in Chapter 4, our explanation of crime is only superficially similar to such accounts of crime as a "social problem." The intellectual roots of our orientation are to be found not in contemporary critiques of American society but in the classical sociological analyses of Émile Durkheim and Robert K. Merton, specifically in their analyses of social deviance and "anomie."

Anomie Theory

THE RISE, FALL, AND REVIVAL OF THE ANOMIE PERSPECTIVE

Core Ideas, Assumptions, and Propositions

The French sociologist Émile Durkheim, a founding figure in sociology, directed attention in the late nineteenth century to the critical role of social factors in explaining human behavior. He also introduced the term "anomie" to refer to a weakening of the normative order in society, and he explored in some detail the consequences of anomie for suicide, a form of deviant behavior that typically is explained with reference to psychological factors.[32]

Our analysis is grounded in the variant of anomie theory associated with the work of the American sociologist Robert K. Merton. Merton combines strategic ideas from Durkheim with insights borrowed from Karl Marx, another founding figure in the social sciences, to produce a provocative and compelling account of the social forces underlying deviant behavior in American society. Although we go beyond Merton's thesis in several important respects (as explained more fully in Chapters 3 and 4), we nevertheless borrow liberally from his arguments and from the anomie research program in sociology and criminology.

Most important, we accept Merton's underlying premise that motivations for crime do not result simply from the flaws, failures, or free choices of individuals. A complete explanation of crime ultimately must consider the sociocultural environments in which people are located. Similar to motivations and desires that promote conformity to norms, deviant and criminal motivations cannot be predicted solely on the basis of assumptions about the "native drives" of the human species.[33] They must be explained, instead, with reference to the particular cultural settings in which people conduct their daily lives. Schopenhauer has called attention to the cultural conditioning of human motivations and desires very nicely in the following passage: "We want what we will, but we don't will what we want."[34]

We also find considerable merit in the observation, basic to both Merton's and Marx's sociological analyses, that strains, tensions, and contradictions are built into concrete forms of social organization. These internal contradictions ultimately provide the impetus for change, and they help account for the dynamic aspects of collective social life.[35] The normal workings of the social system thus may include undesirable forms of behavior, such as crime, just as they include more desirable forms of behavior. Crime does not have to be understood as the product of mysterious or bizarre forces; it can be viewed as an ordinary and predictable response to prevailing sociocultural conditions.[36]

Merton argues that the social system in the United States provides a prime example of a system characterized by internal strain and contradictions. Specifically, he observes an exaggerated emphasis placed on the goal of monetary success in American society, with only a weak emphasis placed on the importance of using socially acceptable means for achieving this goal. This is a normal feature of American culture; as we suggested earlier, it is an integral part of the American Dream. In addition, access to the legitimate means for attaining success remains unequally distributed across the social structure. These cultural and structural

Merton, Durkheim, Marx

conditions produce a pronounced strain toward anomie, that is, a tendency for social norms to lose their regulatory force. Merton suggests that this anomic quality of life creates the high rates of crime and deviance characteristic of the United States. He also proposes that similar sociocultural processes account for the social distribution of crime. The pressures toward anomie, according to Merton, are socially structured. They become progressively more intense at lower levels of the social-class hierarchy because obstacles to the use of the legitimate means for success are greater in the lower classes.

The "Golden Age" of Anomie Theory

Merton's version of anomie theory was introduced to the scholarly community in an article entitled "Social Structure and Anomie," originally published in the *American Sociological Review* in 1938. This article had little immediate impact on the fields of criminology and the sociology of deviance. As one commentator, Stephen Pfohl, has observed, the "essay sat dormant for about fifteen years after its first publication."[37] Then, in the 1950s, anomie theory began to capture the imaginations of influential theorists and researchers. Ambiguities in the original statement of the theory were identified and remedies proposed. Prominent sociologists and criminologists integrated aspects of anomie theory with other criminological ideas to construct explanations of crime and deviance that were both more comprehensive and more precise than Merton's original formulation. The most noteworthy of these efforts were Albert Cohen's *Delinquent Boys* and Richard Cloward and Lloyd Ohlin's *Delinquency and Opportunity.*

Cohen extended Merton's theory to explain how delinquent subcultures emerge from reactions by working-class youth to the middle-class success norms of the school. Cloward and Ohlin joined Merton's theory with the "differential association" perspective on crime developed by Edwin Sutherland to explain how different forms of criminal and deviant activity, including the activities commonly associated with urban youth gangs, result from the failure of lower-class youth to achieve economic success in both the legitimate and the illegitimate "opportunity structures" of the contemporary city.[38] These extensions of Merton's theory highlight the ways in which basic structural conditions can generate subcultures conducive to criminal motivations, thereby explaining the social distribution of crime within a society. Merton himself further advanced the anomie research program by responding to early criticisms of his original theoretical statement and offering expanded and revised versions of the theory in a series of subsequent publications in 1959, 1964, and 1968.[39]

In addition to a growing interest in the theoretical structure of Merton's argument, a large number of empirical studies informed by anomie theory appeared in the late 1950s and throughout the 1960s. The theory was applied to a wide range of deviant behaviors, including crime, delinquency, drug addiction, mental illness, and alcoholism. Researchers interested in macrolevel analysis proposed objective indicators of anomie to explain aggregate crime rates, whereas those interested in individual-level analysis developed social-psychological scales of the subjective experience of confronting an "anomic" environment.[40]

The overall influence of the anomie perspective on the sociological study of deviance during the middle years of the twentieth century is difficult to overstate. Merton's essay "Social Structure and Anomie" and the ideas associated with his perspective more generally were characterized in textbooks as providing the most influential sociological interpretation of deviance during this period.[41] Moreover, the impact of anomie theory was not limited to the academic community. Major policy initiatives such as the Mobilization for Youth program in the 1960s and the War on Poverty more generally were heavily indebted to the general ideas associated with the anomie perspective.[42]

Decline and Revival

Interest in anomie theory, however, dropped markedly in the 1970s and 1980s. Researchers were less likely to draw on the anomie tradition for theoretical guidance, as reflected in the declining number of citations to Merton's work beginning in the early 1970s.[43] In addition, several highly respected scholars directed harsh criticisms at the anomie perspective. In an influential monograph on juvenile delinquency published in 1978, Ruth Kornhauser dismissed the utility of "strain theory," the label given to anomie theory by many criminological theorists at the time, on both theoretical and empirical grounds. She argued that the theory suffers from grievous logical flaws and that its central empirical claims (for example, that the discrepancy between aspirations and achievements is a cause of delinquency) lack support in the research literature. Kornhauser concluded her review of the perspective with the blunt advice to colleagues to turn their attention elsewhere in efforts to explain crime and delinquency.[44]

Anomie theory came under fire from a number of theoretical positions in the 1970s and 1980s, but it would be a mistake to attribute its declining stature during that time to any definitive disconfirmation of its principal claims or to the emergence of a clearly superior alternative. Theoretical dominance in social science reflects not only the intrinsic merits of perspectives and developments internal to intellectual disciplines, but also broader social and political conditions. As the liberal consensus that characterized the postwar era in the United States weakened in the late 1970s, as the welfare state and antipoverty programs came under political fire during the early years of the Reagan administration, as the social movements that provided the political pressure for social welfare policies disappeared, and as crime rates continued to climb, the necessary social supports for a theory universally regarded as advocating liberal social reform as a way to reduce crime withered away.[45]

However, beginning in the late 1980s and continuing to the present, the anomie perspective has enjoyed a resurgence of interest among criminologists. Critical reviews of the earlier critiques, original empirical research applying the perspective, and efforts to elaborate the general theory reflect this interest.[46] Perhaps the resurgence of anomie theory relates partly to the return of an intellectual climate more receptive to its major premises and claims. Given the growing awareness of vexing contemporary social problems—such as homelessness, the urban underclass, glaring and persistent social inequalities amidst affluence, and decay of the inner cities—explanations of social behavior cast in terms of fundamental characteristics of society, rather than individual deficiencies, once again "make sense" to many criminologists.[47]

Regardless of the extent to which anomie theory is in tune with the general intellectual climate, we maintain that this theoretical perspective warrants renewed attention in its own right. The diagnosis of the crime problem advanced by Merton in the 1930s remains highly relevant to contemporary conditions. The most valuable and insightful feature of the anomie perspective, in our view, is that it treats as problematic those enduring cultural and social conditions that liberals and conservatives alike view as potential solutions for crime, such as economic growth, enhanced "competitiveness," and greater equality of opportunity—in short, a renewed commitment to the American Dream.[48]

Unfinished Business

The anomie perspective as developed by Merton and his followers does not, however, provide a fully comprehensive sociological explanation of crime in America. The most conspicuous limitation of Merton's analysis is that it focuses exclusively on one aspect of social structure: inequality in access to the legitimate means for success. As a consequence, it does not explain how specific features of the broader *institutional structure* of society, beyond the stratification system, interrelate to produce the anomic pressures that are responsible for crime.

Anomie theory is thus best regarded as a work in progress. In the words of Albert Cohen, an influential proponent of the anomie perspective, "Merton has laid the groundwork for an explanation of deviance [and crime] on the sociological level, but the task, for the most part, still lies ahead."[49] In the pages that follow, we begin to address the task to which Cohen refers. We explicate the interconnections between culture and institutional structure in contemporary American society and then explore the implications of these interconnections for crime and for efforts at crime control. Before introducing our explanatory framework, we must describe in greater detail the nature of the crime problem in American society.

NOTES

1. Rosoff, Pontell, and Tillman (2003, p. 2). Kenneth Lay's goal of making Enron "the world's leading company" is from the same source (p. 2).

2. Johnson (2004).

3. See Flood and Ivanovich (2004) for a description of the charges against Shilling and other Enron executives. Skilling's disdain for convention is from Tolson (2004). The description of Enron's culture is from Fowler (2002).

4. Rosoff et al. (2003, pp. 1-27) contains an excellent summary of the scandals that beset WorldCom, Global Crossing, Imclone, Adelphia, and Arthur Andersen and Company, the venerable 89-year-old accounting firm, convicted of obstruction of

justice in June 2002 for destroying Enron documents. In 2003 allegations of wide-spread illegal trading in mutual funds hit the headlines (Valdmanis, 2003). In March 2004, the famous "gracious living" expert Martha Stewart was convicted of lying to federal investigators about receiving inside information on a stock transaction (ABCNEWS.com, 2004).

5. *Columbia Encyclopedia* (1993).

6. Sullivan (1992).

7. Truell (1995); *New York Times (1990).*

8. Clines (1993, p. 9).

9. Tolson (2004).

10. Erikson (1966, p. 21).

11. Black (1984); on crime as a form of social control in illegal markets, see Reuter (1984).

12. International comparisons are from Barclay and Tavares (2002).

13. The authors have calculated the percentages from the General Social Survey (GSS) data for 2002. GSS data are from biannual surveys of nationally representative samples of American adults conducted by the National Opinion Research Center. For information on the GSS, see http://www.norc.org.

14. Marriott (1995).

15. For evidence concerning fear of crime and neighborhood satisfaction, see Skogan (1990, pp. 83-84). The reference to the Rodney King case is from Chapman (1992). In a subsequent federal trial, two of the police officers in this case were found guilty of violating King's civil rights.

16. Adler (1983, p. xix).

17. Harrison and Beck (2003); Mauer (2003).

18. Calculated by the authors from 2002 GSS data.

19. For a general discussion of the view that "evil" outcomes must have "evil" causes and of alternative perspectives, see Nisbet (1971, pp. 9-14).

20. Adams (1931) has been referred to as "the historian of the American Dream" by his biographer Allan Nevins (1968; see p. 68n for the reference to the publisher's resistance to Adams's preferred title).

21. Hearn (1977, pp. 18, 192).

22. Hearn (1977, p. 201).

23. Long (1985, p. 196).

24. Merton (1968, p. 200).

25. Schwartz (1994b, p. 259) invokes this adage in a similar context in his discussion of the "debasing of education".

26. Ewen and Hart (2003, p. 16). Figures on working mothers and child-care arrangements are from U.S. Bureau of the Census (2003, p. 359, Table 359, and p. 373, Table 570).

27. The notion that persistent economic disadvantage reflects the betrayal of the American Dream is developed at length by Ropers (1991).

28. Statistics on income distribution are from the U.S. Bureau of the Census (2004).

29. Levy (1988, p. 2); see also Turner and Musick (1985, p. 178); Schwarz (1995-96), and U.S. Bureau of the Census (2004).

30. Turner and Musick (1985, p. 181) discuss historical patterns in the distribution of wealth. For documentation of growth in the concentration of wealth in the 1980s and 1990s, see Wolff (1995). The Federal Reserve estimate of wealth distribution is from Koretz (2003:28).

31. Schur (1969). See also Derber (1992, 1996).

32. Durkheim ([1893] 1964a, [1897] 1966).

33. Merton (1968, p. 175).

34. Quoted in Johnson (1991, p. 26).

35. Merton (1968, p. 176).

36. See Orru (1990, p. 232).

37. Merton (1938); Pfohl (1985, p. 226).

38. Cohen (1955); Cloward and Ohlin (1960); see also Lilly, Cullen, and Ball (1989, pp. 71–75). The central premise of differential association theory is that people learn criminal motivations and behaviors through exposure to norms and beliefs that favor law violation. See Sutherland (1947) for an early statement of the perspective and Chapter 3 for an expanded discussion and critique of Sutherland's theory.

39. Merton (1959, 1964, 1968).

40. See Clinard (1964) for an appraisal of early work in these areas.

41. Gibbons (1992, p. 110). See also Turner (1978, p. 83).

42. Liska (1987, pp. 51–54).

43. Cole (1975).

44. Kornhauser (1978, p. 180).

45. Material in this paragraph is drawn from Rosenfeld (1989).

46. See, for example, Adler and Laufer (1995), Agnew (1992), Bernard (1984), Farnworth and Lieber (1989), Featherstone and Deflem (2003), Menard (1995), Messner (1988), and Passas and Agnew (1997).

47. For a general discussion of how criminological theories reflect the larger social context, see Lilly, Cullen, and Ball (1989, pp. 77, 81).

48. See Samuelson (1992) for an insightful discussion of the belief that prosperity is a panacea for social problems.

49. Cohen (1985, p. 233).

2

By Any Means Necessary
Serious Crime in America

It is needless to waste words in painting the situation in our
country today. The headlines of any metropolitan newspaper
any day do so only too clearly. Crime of the most desperate
sort is so rampant that unless a robbery runs into six figures or
a murder is outstandingly brutal or intriguing, we no longer
even read below the headings.

JAMES TRUSLOW ADAMS,

(HISTORIAN, 1929)[1]

People in America's biggest cities aren't concerned about a hijacked
plane hitting their neighborhood as much as they are on edge about
drive-by shootings and stabbings on their front lawns.

WILLIAM BRATTON,

(LOS ANGELES CHIEF OF POLICE, 2004)[2]

On September 11, 2001, the United States and the world were shocked by
terrorist attacks on the World Trade Center in New York and the Pentagon
in Washington, DC. Immediately after the attacks, President George W. Bush
declared war on terrorism. Over two years later, in January 2004, the President
emphasized the continuing priority of that war.

I remember talking to the country after September the 11th,
and reminding people that this would be a different kind of war we
faced.... By our will, by our steadfast determination, by our courage,
we will prevail in the war—first war of the 21st century.

The President went on to praise the coordination among different levels of government in the fight against terrorism, and announced a budget proposal for more spending on homeland security.

> In the United States, where the war begun (sic), we will continue our vital work to protecting (sic) American people, by protecting our ports and borders and safeguarding infrastructure, preparing for the worst. ...
> I can't tell you how pleased I am with the coordination now between the federal government, the state government, and local governments for preparing our homeland. I'm going to submit a budget to Congress next month, which will include spending of $30 billion for homeland security. That's—more than $30 billion—almost three times the amount that we were spending prior to September the 11th, 2001.
> We understand our obligation in Washington. Our obligation is never to forget what happened on September the 11th. And our obligation is to support the homeland security people, those on the front lines, to prepare for a potential threat.[3]

A week before President Bush announced his resolve to continue the war against terrorism, police chiefs from across the United States convened in Los Angeles to address the problem of gang violence in America's cities. In his opening address, Los Angeles Chief William Bratton stressed that his city was in more immediate danger from gang violence than a terrorist attack: "This is what's killing young people here. This is what has the potential to kill many cities." Bratton urged a "national wake-up call" on gang crime, calling it a "sleeping tiger" that had been left to local areas to contend with without adequate federal resources or coordination.[4]

It is pointless, in our view, to debate whether terrorism or street crime poses a greater danger to Americans. Clearly, both threaten lives, generate fear, and impose restrictions on day-to-day conduct. Nonetheless, it is informative to compare the risks of terrorist violence with those of more prosaic but equally deadly sources of intentional violence.[5] Consider the 2001 terrorist attacks on the United States. The FBI took special pains in its Uniform Crime Reports for 2001 to distinguish the homicides resulting from the attacks on the Pentagon and New York City from the other approximately 16,000 homicides that occurred nationwide that year. The reported homicide count and rate for New York City in 2001 excluded the 2,823 World Trade Center victims. How would New York's picture of lethal violence have appeared had those deaths been included in the city's homicide rate? Obviously, the picture would have been far worse. The city's official homicide rate of 9 per 100,000 population would have increased nearly five-fold to a rate of 44 per 100,000—a disturbingly high but not unparalleled rate, about the same as the homicide rates in New Orleans, Detroit, and Washington, DC, but lower than Gary, Indiana's rate of 79 per 100,000.[6] Millions of Americans live with rates of "everyday" violence rivaling the worst terrorist incident in U.S. history.

In view of the pervasiveness of violent crime throughout urban America, Americans can easily suppose that the social conditions of advanced societies naturally promote a high degree of criminal violence. However, this understandable supposition runs directly counter to a leading theoretical perspective and a sizable research literature on long-term trends in crime rates. This body of work, referred to as the modernization thesis, reveals that Western societies exhibit levels of interpersonal violence today that are considerably lower than they were centuries ago. To explain this long-term decline in interpersonal violence, historian Ted Robert Gurr offers the idea of a "civilizing process" (a notion originally introduced by Norbert Elias). As Western civilization has progressed, Gurr argues, internal and external controls on the overt display of violence have increased markedly, and humanistic values have become more widely accepted.[7]

The relationship between modernization and crime also has been explored in quantitative, cross-sectional analyses based on samples of contemporary nations at varying stages of development. Consistent with the historical research, cross-sectional studies provide no support for the notion that a high level of criminal violence is a natural feature of the social landscape of modern industrial and postindustrial societies.[8] Comparisons of the developed societies of the world prompt the question of why rates of serious crime are so surprisingly high in one of them: the United States. We address this basic question about crime in this book.

In the present chapter, we review international statistics on two of the most serious types of conventional crime: homicide and robbery. We consider the case for American exceptionalism with respect to not only the *level* of serious crime but also the *form* of and the *social response* to crime. We then consider the extent of white-collar crime in the United States. Although we lack reliable estimates of the volume of this kind of offending for international comparisons, clear evidence indicates widespread and costly white-collar crime. Moreover, both types of crime—"suite" crime as well as "street" crime—have devastating consequences for both those who are victimized and those who live in fear of becoming crime victims.

Chapter 2 closes with qualitative descriptions drawn from news accounts of how individuals and communities cope with crime conditions that in many respects parallel those during wartime. In their portrayal of personal struggles with crime and fear, the vignettes put a human face on the official statistics on crime in America. These descriptions also reveal an institutional struggle with crime in many American communities, as businesses, churches, schools, families, and law enforcement agencies find themselves under siege and, in their weakened condition, end up contributing to even higher levels of neighborhood disorganization and crime. This focus on the interplay between crime and social institutions sets the stage for the assessment and reformulation of sociological explanations of crime in Chapter 3.

CROSS-NATIONAL COMPARISONS OF CRIME

Homicide and Robbery Rates in International Context

Comparisons of the crime rates of different nations must be made with considerable caution. Both the reporting of crimes to the police and police recording practices differ from one nation to another, as do procedures for reporting crime statistics to international agencies. Most important, different nations employ varying definitions of crime. Although these problems are less likely to affect comparisons across developed nations for the most serious offenses, such as those under consideration here, it is best to treat small differences in crime rates between nations as unreliable, especially when comparisons are based on data for a single year.[9]

With these cautions in mind, it is instructive to compare recorded levels of homicide and robbery in the United States with levels observed in other advanced nations. Figure 2.1 reports the U.S. homicide rate, along with those of fifteen other post-industrial nations. These data come from the vital statistics on causes of death. The source for the United States is the National Center for Health Statistics (NCHS). The homicide data for other nations are from the World Health Organization (WHO), which defines homicide as "death by injury purposely inflicted by others."[10] The data in Figure 2.1 are quite striking, revealing the United States as a clear outlier among highly developed nations in its level of lethal violence. The U.S. rate of 5.9 homicides per 100,000 population more than doubles Finland's rate of 2.6 per 100,000 population, the next highest among the nations presented in the sample. It is almost 5 times the average rate of the other nations.

Figure 2.2 reports robbery rates for the same 16-nation sample. The robbery data for the United States come from the FBI's *Uniform Crime Reports* (UCR), while the statistics for the remaining nations are from the International Criminal Police Organization (Interpol), which defines robbery as "violent theft." This definition accords with the general classification of robberies in the United States and elsewhere as thefts (including attempts) accompanied by force or the threat of force.[11] The data on robbery rates displayed in Figure 2.2 reveal that France has the highest robbery rate among the nations listed, followed by England and Wales, and then the United States. The U.S rate of 145.9 robberies per 100,000 residents thus ranks near, albeit not at, the top, and is well above the average value of 89.8.

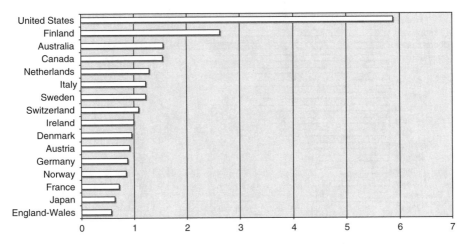

FIGURE 2.1 Homicide Rates in 16 Nations, 1996–2000 (homicides per 100,000 population)

The Form of Criminal Behavior

As the robbery statistics indicate, the case for American exceptionalism in levels of crime should not be overstated. Even with respect to homicide, some nations exhibit levels that exceed those of the United States. Homicide rates in the Russian Federation have surpassed those of the United States in recent years, and several South American nations have consistently exhibited very high homicide rates. Rates for certain property crimes are not exceptionally high in the United States when compared with other advanced societies.[12] However, when comparing the crime situation across nations, we must consider the *form* of criminal activity, as well as the level of crime. What seems to be most distinctive about crime in the United States is its unrestrained and dangerous character. In other words, whether the offense involves violence or theft, it is more likely to take the form of crime "by any means necessary."

David Bayley provides an amusing and instructive illustration of ways in which property crimes might differ across societies in form, even if not in frequency, in his analysis of the role of "propriety" in Japanese society.[13] Bayley cites the case of a burglar who was apprehended fleeing an apartment. The burglar was caught because he had stopped to put his shoes on. Why did he have his shoes off in the first place? In Japan, it is customary to remove one's shoes when entering a private home, especially if the home has the traditional flooring of woven straw. The burglar had to cross such a floor to get at a bureau that he wanted to ransack; thus, in accordance with Japanese notions of propriety, he first removed his shoes. Evidently, the Japanese sense of propriety affects even the way burglars conduct their illegal activities. It is hard to imagine the typical American burglar exhibiting similar restraint when committing his or her crimes. Of course, Swedish or Canadian burglars may also find the Japanese sense of propriety in crime somewhat demanding. Nevertheless, the general point is

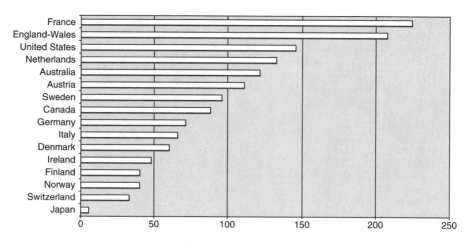

FIGURE 2.2 Robbery Rates in 16 Nations, 2000–2002
(robberies per 100,000 population)

consistent with the cross-national evidence on crime: The more serious the offense, the greater the potential or actual harm to the victim, and the more unrestrained its character, the more the United States tends to diverge from other advanced industrial societies.[14]

Going back to Figure 2.2, the data show the robbery rate in England and Wales to be higher than that in the United States (207.4 vs. 145.9 per 100,000). But consider the form: Robberies in the United States are nearly 10 times more likely to be carried out with a firearm (41 percent of robberies) than those in England and Wales (4.5 percent). Being robbed is an unpleasant and often frightening experience wherever it occurs. Being robbed at gunpoint is cause for special concern, because the robbery is much more likely to end with the victim's death if the weapon is used and the victim is injured. The form of criminal behavior matters a great deal when comparing the crime situation across nations, even when the comparisons are limited to the same offense type. Violent crime in the United States is more likely to assume a deadly form.[15]

The Social Response to Crime

Finally, to fully appreciate a nation's crime problem, one must consider not only the level and form of illegal activity but also the *social response* to crime. The exceptionally high rates of homicide and the relatively high levels of robbery reported for the United States in Figures 2.1 and 2.2 are particularly remarkable when considered in the context of a major development in American punishment practices over recent decades: the reliance on incarceration as a crime-control measure to a degree that is unheard of elsewhere. The United States incarcerates its population at a rate five to ten times that of other developed nations: 85 incarcerated per 100,000 population in France, 139 per 100,000 in England-Wales, and 702 per 100,000 in the United States in 2002.[16] How much of the difference in the robbery rates between the United States and the other two nations can be attributed to the vast difference in their respective incarceration rates?

The massive scale of incarceration in the United States has almost surely depressed the recorded robbery rate and the rates of other serious offenses below what they would be in the absence of such policies, which are often cited approvingly by politicians and governmental officials for just that reason.[17] However, as Elliott Currie has argued, incarceration does not solve the "real crime problem" but merely shifts the pool of criminals away from the public domain, where they can be counted, to institutional settings, where their criminality lies hidden. Incarceration "hides" criminality in two important ways. Most obviously, the many crimes committed in prisons never enter into the official crime records. In addition, incarceration limits the opportunity for the criminal propensities of prisoners to become manifested in criminal acts. This, of course, forms a large part of the rationale for imprisonment—to incapacitate offenders—and it is a legitimate policy objective. Yet, to the extent that incapacitation is the operative goal of imprisonment, high levels of incarceration make the recorded crime rate a problematic indicator of the socially generated degree of *criminality*.

To illustrate this point, consider the analogy of disease.[18] If we were interested in assessing the extent to which social or environmental conditions produce physical illness, we would not systematically exclude from our count of diseased persons all those who have been admitted to hospitals. They are precisely the persons who have been most affected by disease. Yet when we use the officially recorded level of crimes to reflect the criminality in society without adjusting for the size of the incarcerated population, we essentially do the same thing. A full picture of the criminogenic pressures in a society thus requires that levels of both crime and punishment be taken into account. When levels of serious crime are considered in combination with the rate at which persons are incarcerated, the United States stands far apart from all other highly developed nations.

Gun-Related Crime

An important question underlying the commanding predominance of the United States over other advanced nations in serious crime, especially homicide, involves the use of firearms: How much does the greater availability of guns in the United States account for the difference in crime rates? Rates of gun ownership are much higher in America than in other Western nations. An analysis of the results of national victimization surveys conducted in nine Western industrialized societies between 1995 and 1997 found that guns were present in 49 percent of U.S. households. The next closest rate of household gun prevalence was in Switzerland, where guns were reported in 36 percent of all households. However, we must recognize that firearm ownership in Switzerland is associated with military service. Handgun ownership showed similar patterns. The United States exhibited the highest percentage of households reporting a handgun, 25 percent, followed once again by Switzerland at 14 percent. No other nation in the survey had a handgun ownership rate higher than 9 percent.[19]

Although most homicides in the United States are committed with a gun, and most gun-related homicides are committed with a handgun, determining precisely how much of the U.S. homicide rate can be attributed to the widespread availability of firearms remains difficult.[20] For our purposes, however, such a determination is unnecessary because even if all of the gun-related homicides were eliminated from the U.S. homicide rate, the United States would still have a non-gun-related homicide rate higher than the total homicide rates of most other developed nations.

We can illustrate this point with some simple calculations. In 2002, 66.7 percent of the homicides in the United States were committed with a gun. The remaining 33.3 percent were committed with other weapons (usually a knife) or without a weapon. Therefore, the non-gun-related homicide rate in the United States was 33.3 percent of the total rate of 5.6, or 1.86 per 100,000 population.[21] This level of lethal violence committed without a firearm is greater than the *overall* homicide rates of all but one of the other nations (Finland) displayed in Figure 2.1. For example, it is over three times the rate of 0.56 homicides per 100,000 population for England-Wales. As do many other nations, British law and custom strongly discourage the private ownership of firearms. Yet, even if no homicides in England and Wales were committed with a firearm, restricted access to guns could not explain the sizable difference between the American non-gun-related homicide rate and the total homicide rate in Britain.

We do not propose that the huge supply of guns in the United States—which at well over 200 million amounts to the largest private arsenal in the world—has no bearing on its rate of lethal violence. Along with other criminologists, we suspect that guns may be one factor that, in combination with others, helps explain the high levels of criminal violence in the U.S.[22] However, we want to call attention to the equally sobering point that even if none of these weapons were ever used in another killing, the United States would still be left with one of the highest rates of homicide among the advanced nations.

The response of the Japanese public illustrates the cultural complexities underlying the guns-crime relationship when, on a Halloween night, a 16-year-old exchange student from Japan was shot to death by a homeowner near Baton Rouge, Louisiana. The student knocked on the door of a house where he mistakenly thought a party was being held. He was shot when he continued to approach the owner, apparently not understanding the command to "freeze." The killing itself shocked the Japanese. Many were even more appalled, however, by the subsequent acquittal of the American homeowner on the grounds of self-defense. In the words of a professor of American cultural studies at the University of Tokyo, "I think for the Japanese the most remarkable thing is that you could get a jury of Americans together, and they could conclude that shooting someone before you even talked to him was reasonable behavior."[23]

This account suggests that the Japanese do not attribute the killing of the exchange student, and presumably other homicides in the United States, simply to the availability of firearms. Rather, they look to deeper cultural differences for an explanation of the striking contrast between Japan and America in both the number of lethal weapons in private hands and the level of interpersonal violence. Japanese commentators characterized the events surrounding the killing, the plea of "self-defense" against an unarmed teenager in a Halloween costume, and the jury's verdict of not guilty as a reflection of an "out-of-control" society in which people are allowed to shoot one another with little or no provocation. According to the American studies professor quoted earlier, the cultural significance of the Baton Rouge case is that Americans and Japanese "go by different rules." "We are more civilized," she concludes. "We rely on words."

One does not have to endorse the invidious claim that the Japanese are "more civilized" to concur with the general sentiment expressed in these remarks that the exceptional level of lethal violence in the United States involves something more than the quantity, availability, or lethality of firearms. An adequate explanation of gun-related violence must account for those qualities of the cultural "rules" that make Americans unusually willing to deploy the means of final resort in dealing with perceived threats and interpersonal disputes.

Has It Always Been This Way?

International comparisons of serious crime, and especially lethal violence, raise the question of whether the relatively high rates observed for the United States are recent in origin or have persisted over a long period of time. Indeed, perhaps the distinctiveness of the United States in Figure 2.1 as the clear leader in homicide rates among the sample of advanced nations is a fluke, a mere reflection of an unusually high rate in the particular year represented.

This is clearly not the case. Since early in the twentieth century and perhaps as far back as the middle of the nineteenth century, rates of lethal criminal violence in the United States have far exceeded those in other modern industrial societies. The persistence of comparatively high levels of homicide in the United States is documented in Figure 2.3 for the period 1900–2002.[24] The data for the earliest years of the period are of questionable reliability because of technical inadequacies in the collection of mortality data.[25] With this qualification in mind, several observations can be drawn from Figure 2.3 regarding change and persistence in levels of homicide in the United States during the twentieth century.

The first is the considerable variability in homicide rates over the period. The level of homicide approximately doubled from 1910 to the mid-1930s, peaking at over nine homicides per 100,000 population in the latter years. Homicide rates then declined to fewer than five per 100,000 population during the 1950s and early 1960s. They then began a second period of pronounced increase, comparable to that at the beginning of the century. The second observation to be made about these changes, however, is that they occur around a high and apparently stationary base rate. The mean level of homicide of 6.8 per 100,000 population over the period usually exceeds the highest rates of other industrial nations. In fact, with few exceptions, the lowest annual rates of homicide recorded in the United States over the past century are greater than the highest rates found in other industrial societies.[26]

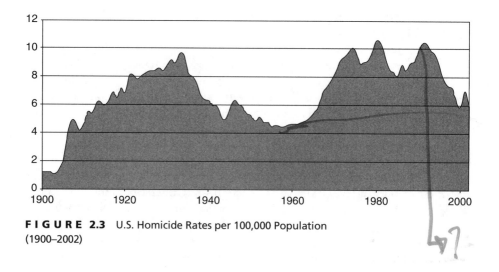

FIGURE 2.3 U.S. Homicide Rates per 100,000 Population (1900–2002)

Figure 2.3 reveals one final important characteristic of U.S. trends in serious criminal violence during the last decades of the twentieth century: After peaking around 1980 and then again in the early 1990s, the rates fell rather sharply to levels not seen since the late 1960s. The story for robbery is similar to that for homicide. In fact, rates of serious crime of all types, property as well as violent, decreased during the 1990s, and the declines were registered in data from crime victims in the National Crime Victimization Survey (NCVS) as well as the UCR data from police agencies.

The crime decline of the 1990s, coming as it did after a period of marked increase during the previous decade, caught many academic experts and social commentators off guard, and a firm consensus does not exist regarding the underlying causes. However, when placed in historical and comparative perspective, the most recent crime decline does not undermine our basic argument regarding the sources of high rates of serious crime in America. Although historical changes in rates of homicide and other serious crimes in the United States are far from insignificant, and even allowing for considerable measurement error in the available statistics, it appears that the conditions contributing to the levels and forms of these crimes, and to mass incarceration as a response, are related to enduring patterns of social organization that distinguish our society from other advanced industrial societies.

Race and Criminal Violence

A final factor that might explain why rates of serious crime are higher in the United States than in other advanced nations is population heterogeneity. The United States is more ethnically and racially diverse than most other industrialized nations, and large differences in violent crime rates exist among racial and ethnic groups within American society. In particular, African-Americans are overrepresented among both the victims and offenders in incidents of criminal violence. For example, blacks compose about 13 percent of the U.S. population but accounted for 48 percent of the 13,864 homicide victims in 2002 with known race. The homicide victimization rate among black Americans is more than six times that among white Americans. Homicide is the sixth leading cause of death among all African-Americans; it is the leading cause of death among young African-American males. Homicides contributed to fully 49 percent of all the deaths in 2001 among black males 20 to 24 years old. The proportion of deaths from homicide among white men of the same age was 11 percent.[27]

We cannot think of a more alarming set of social indicators in the United States than these measures of risk for lethal violence among black Americans, especially young black males. However, as high as they are, levels of homicide victimization among black Americans do not explain fully the differences in homicide rates between the United States and other developed societies. The victimization rate of 2.9 homicides per 100,000 population among whites only exceeds the *total* homicide rate for all other nations in Figure 2.2.

Given the overwhelmingly intra-racial character of homicide (over 90 percent of all homicides involve victims and offenders of the same race), we may assume that these differences in homicide victimization reflect similar differences in offending between blacks and whites in the United States. Available information on the racial characteristics of homicide suspects supports this assumption. The rate of homicide offending among blacks is about 6.5 times the rate for whites. Nonetheless, the white homicide offending rate in 2002 of 2.3 per 100,000 population is higher than the homicide rates of all other developed nations shown in Figure 2.2, with the exception of Finland. Racial differences notwithstanding, then, with respect to both offending and victimization, levels of lethal violence among white Americans are strikingly high when viewed in cross-national perspective.[28]

The importance of racial differences in crime within the United States, either as a theoretical issue for criminological inquiry or as a social problem with a particularly profound impact on racially disadvantaged groups, should not be minimized. (We discuss this issue in greater detail in Chapter 4.) For that matter, neither should we ignore the relationship between the extraordinary supply of weapons in private hands and the exceptionally high levels of interpersonal violence in America. The primary analysis of this book, however, focuses on variation in rates of crime at the level of nation-states, and a careful examination of the international statistics on violent crime and punishment suggests that the distinctiveness of the United States in comparison with other developed nations cannot be easily explained away by recent trends in crime, the greater availability of firearms, or the disproportionate involvement in crime by minority groups. Moreover, some of the most serious acts of criminal offending rarely involve the use of guns and are committed by persons in positions of high status that typically are occupied by members of the dominant racial group. We now turn to these crimes committed by the well-to-do, the so-called white-collar crimes.

WHITE-COLLAR CRIMES

You are safer on the subway than in any country club in America, especially when it comes to the danger of corruption.

The best way to rob a bank is to own one.[29]

Prevalence and Costs of White-Collar Crime

White-collar crimes, generally defined as crimes committed by persons against the organizations for which they work (embezzlement, for example) or on behalf of those organizations (for instance, price fixing), occur with great frequency in the United States and result in significant individual and collective harm. Unfortunately, we lack reliable information on differences across societies in the rates of white-collar offending. However, several studies have shown that white-collar criminality is common in American society. A pioneering study by Edwin Sutherland, who coined the term "white-collar crime," revealed a pattern of widespread illegality and repeat offending on the part of the 70 largest companies in the United States. Each of the corporations had at least one adverse decision against it by a regulatory agency or court over a twenty-year period, and the firms averaged 14 adverse decisions. Nearly all of the corporations were "recidivists" in the sense that they committed violations on a repeated basis.

The findings of Sutherland's research, conducted during the 1940s, have been confirmed in subsequent investigations of corporate offending. A 1980 study of nearly 600 major corporations found that 60 percent had federal cases brought against them over a two-year period; over 40 percent had two or more actions initiated against them over the same period. A more recent investigation by journalists found that civil or criminal actions for serious misconduct were filed against 23 percent of the nation's 500 largest companies over a 10-year period. Fourteen of the 25 largest firms incurred civil or criminal penalties in excess of $50,000. Because these figures reflect legal actions or adverse decisions against corporations, they understate by a substantial margin actual levels of corporate crime, much of which goes undetected.[30]

Asking people if they have been the victims of illegal business activities provides an alternative way of measuring the prevalence of white-collar crime. A survey conducted in the early 1990s asked a nationally representative sample of Americans whether they had been the victims of fraud, defined as "the misrepresentation of facts and the deliberate intent to deceive with the promise of goods, services, or other financial benefits that in fact do not exist or that were never intended to be provided." Just under one-third of the respondents said they had been victims of attempted or completed fraud.[31]

White-collar offending is not only prevalent but also quite serious. The aggregate impact of white-collar offending is impossible to measure with any degree of precision, but scholars estimate that the costs of these crimes exceed those of conventional street crimes, which are themselves quite high at just under $18 billion a year.[32] Rosoff and colleagues estimate that white-collar crimes exact a monetary toll of $250 billion a year, or about *fourteen times* the estimated yearly costs of robbery, burglary, assault, and other street crimes. A single white-collar crime, or a cluster of related offenses, can have a staggering monetary impact—or, from the offender's perspective, an immense financial return. For example, taxpayers spent an estimated $3.4 billion to pay off the debts of Lincoln Savings and Loan, a fraudulent savings institution run by Charles Keating during the 1980s. The losses associated with all bank robberies in the United States amount to $35 million a year, about 1 percent of the costs of the Keating scandal.[33]

It is now generally accepted that white-collar crimes have an enormous economic impact on consumers and taxpayers. However, the usual aggregate calculation or their costs obscures the effects of white-collar crimes on individual victims. Sometimes the direct consequences for individuals of white-collar offending are quite small, precisely because there are so many victims. A price-fixing scheme that generates millions of dollars in illegal profits to business owners may cost individual consumers only a few pennies more in higher prices. The impact of this kind of offense is more fully reflected in the number of victims rather than in the economic harm done to each one.

Yet it would be a mistake to minimize the individual impact of white-collar criminality. White-collar crimes can result in the loss of savings, homes, and jobs. Recall from Chapter 1 that Enron officials refused to permit employees to withdraw their savings from the company's retirement plan at the same time company executives were cashing in their Enron stock holdings for millions. By the time employees were finally allowed to sell the stock in their 401K retirement accounts, Enron stock prices had plummeted. A 64-year-old office manager's account went from $700,000 to $20,000; a 54-year-old sheet metal worker lost all but $4,500 of life savings once valued at $450,000.[34] Retail workers in some of the nation's largest and best-known discount chains have accused their supervisors of illegally altering payroll records to increase profits. Managers uneasy with the practice, known as "shaving time," have been threatened with the loss of their own jobs if they refuse to doctor payroll accounts. An individual worker may lose only a few hours a week to time shaving, but that may be a considerable sum to a retail clerk earning $8-10 an hour. The supervisors also may have a lot to lose if they refuse orders to shave time. As a lawyer who brought a successful suit against the practice observes: "They have no job security at all, and they want to keep their toehold in the lower middle class, and they'll often do whatever is necessary to do it."[35]

Violent White-Collar Crime

There should be no difficulty at all in appreciating the harmful consequences for individual victims of white-collar crimes that cause disease, injury, or death. However, no clear and widely accepted standards for determining whether a white-collar crime is a "violent crime" exist. Most Americans would agree that an elderly woman who loses her savings in a fraudulent investment scheme is the victim of a crime. We seem to have more difficulty viewing the coal miner who develops black lung disease or the child who is injured while playing with an unsafe toy as crime victims. Yet considerable evidence indicates that so-called nonviolent white-collar criminals kill and maim more people each year in the United States than do violent street criminals.

In 2002, 5,524 workers were killed on the job in the United States. Another 23,900 deaths resulted from unsafe or defective merchandise. Defective products or dangerous working conditions seriously injure or sicken several million people per year. The Consumer Product Safety Commission recorded about 33 million nonfatal injuries from consumer products in 2002. (This figure excludes injuries from firearms, which are not covered by the CPSC.) The U.S. Department of Labor counted 4.4 million job-related injuries and 295,000 illness cases (from poisoning, skin disease, respiratory illness, for example) in 2002.[36] Even if only one of every ten such incidents were the result of criminal offenses or violations, the number would be far greater than that of yearly deaths and injuries from homicides and serious assaults in the United States. In fact, 10 percent is a conservative estimate of the deaths and injuries related to unsafe jobs, products, and environments attributable to white-collar crime. Studies have shown that as many as one-third to one-half of job-related accidents are the result of crimes or violations by employers.[37] When combined with the evidence on the economic impact of white-collar crime, such findings have prompted a leading analyst of white-collar crime to conclude that "by virtually any criterion . . . , white-collar crime is our most serious crime problem."[38]

Social Response

As with street crime, we should consider the social response to white-collar crime, as well as its level and forms. Headline-making reports of huge fines and lengthy prison sentences for high-profile corporate criminals could lead to the conclusion that the social response to white-collar offending is highly punitive. That conclusion would be incorrect, especially in cases resulting in serious injury and death. Very few such cases end up in the criminal courts; the vast majority, when any action is taken at all, result in citations and fines for violating workplace health and safety standards. A visit to the website (www.osha.gov) of the Occupational Health and Safety Administration (OSHA), responsible for enforcing those standards, offers an illuminating view of the tepid social response to so-called violent white-collar crime.

OSHA publishes and periodically updates a series of accident reports it terms "Fatal Facts," which "were selected as representative of fatalities caused by improper work practices."[39] The reports are categorized by cause, such as "crushed by falling wall," "crushed by falling machinery," "trench cave-in," "caught in machinery," "explosion," "asphyxiation," and "electrocution." In one case, a 32-year-old pipe layer was crushed and killed while

> installing storm drain pipes in a trench, approximately 20-30 feet long, 12-13 feet deep and 5-6 feet wide. The side walls consisted of unstable

soil undermined by sand and water. There was 3-5 feet of water in the north end of the trench and 5-6 inches of water in the south end. At the time of the accident, a backhoe was being used to clear the trench. The west wall of the trench collapsed. . . .

In another case, a 28-year-old welder died from burns after he had

entered a steel pipe (24 inch diameter) to grind a bad weld at a valve about 30 feet from the entry point. Before he entered, other crew members decided to add oxygen to the pipe near the bad weld. He had been grinding intermittently for about five minutes when a fire broke out enveloping his clothing.

The only thing unusual about these "accidents" is that they resulted in citations for "willful" violations of workplace standards. After inspecting a work site, OSHA may issue the employer one or more citations for violations of varying degrees of seriousness. The most serious is a "willful violation," defined as "a violation that the employer intentionally and knowingly commits." OSHA may also cite an employer for a "serious" violation of standards "where there is a substantial probability that death or physical harm could result and that the employer knew, or should have known, of the hazard." OSHA also issues citations for repeated violations, for failure to correct prior violations, and for violations that "probably would not cause death or serious physical harm." During fiscal 2003 OSHA undertook 39,798 workplace inspections, and issued 83,562 citations for violations of standards. Of these, only 196, or 0.1 percent, were issued for willful violations. Most of the remainder, however, were for serious violations.

OSHA does not have the authority to bring criminal charges against employers who violate health and safety rules. It must refer cases for criminal action to the Justice Department. Since OSHA's creation in 1972, 200,000 workers have been killed on the job. OSHA has referred just 151 cases (less than 0.1%) to the Justice Department, and federal prosecutors acted on fewer than half of those referrals. According to a Pulitzer-Prize-winning *New York Times* study, between 1982 and 2002 OSHA investigated 1,242 incidents in which workers died as the result of willful health and safety violations. OSHA declined to seek prosecution in 93 percent of those cases.[40] Even the relatively few cases that were prosecuted and ended in convictions brought impressively light punishment. Under federal law, causing the death of an employee through willful violation of health and safety standards is a misdemeanor carrying a maximum sentence of six months in jail and fine of $70,000. By contrast, harassing a burro on federal lands carries a maximum jail term of one year.[41]

The lax punishment of employers whose violations of health and safety regulations result in significant injury or death to workers stands in stark contrast to the harsh response to street criminals. Why are the criminal penalties for white-collar offenders so gentle in comparison with those for other offenders? Why is the criminal law so rarely invoked when employers violate, sometimes routinely, regulations to promote the health and safety of their employees? Many postulate that powerful groups can influence the political and legal process to protect their interests. When asked for his reaction to new proposals to upgrade willful violations by employers that result in death from a misdemeanor to a felony, a representative of the U.S. Chamber of Commerce stated flatly, "Obviously, we're not going to support the expansion of criminal penalties."[42]

But lenient treatment of white-collar criminals reflects something more fundamental about the nature of American society and culture than the simple (and somewhat circular) logic that more powerful groups are able to promote their interests at the expense of less powerful groups. The same social forces that lead to high levels of serious crime also produce the contrasting social responses to street crime and suite crime. The American Dream, as we shall see, is implicated in both crime and punishment in the United States. The present point is that the massive penal response to street crime and the indulgent attitude toward suite crime both conceal criminality, in one case behind bars, in the other behind bureaucratic regulations and civil penalties that make it appear as though no crime has been committed.

SERIOUS CRIME AND THE QUALITY OF LIFE

The summary counts, rates, and comparative figures on crime and the costs of crime presented so far are indispensable for describing, and ultimately explaining, the crime problem in the United States. However, the quantitative data alone do not adequately capture the social reality of serious crime. A different, but no less important or real, set of facts about the personal and social impacts of crime reveal another, more qualitative, dimension of experiences with crime. We conclude this chapter, therefore, by supplementing the quantitative indicators of the crime problem with qualitative descriptions of the fear, anger, frustration, and desperation that form the texture of day-to-day living with serious crime.

Taking Precautions by Any Means Necessary

Although, as we noted in Chapter 1, the fear of crime is widespread in America, people take precautions against crime in all urban industrial societies. For example, in a survey of 15 nations conducted in 2000, respondents were presented with a list of common measures to protect against burglary. The list included burglar alarm, special door locks, window grilles, watchdog, high fence, caretaker/security guard, and formal neighborhood watch scheme. The United States exhibited a relatively high percentage of respondents reporting the use of these measures, ranking in the top third for all but the "high fence" measure. Although the United States did not rank at the top for any one measure (the highest ranking was second, for having a watchdog), the rankings across the list were consistently higher than average.[43]

These survey data effectively describe what might be considered the normal level of fear characteristic of everyday life in most modern societies. What the figures do not reveal, however, are the acute pockets of fear found in the high-crime neighborhoods of nearly all large American cities but in few other places in the industrialized world—except during wartime. The comparative statistics also do not distinguish the standard protective measures undertaken by urban dwellers in all nations (such as avoiding certain streets or areas after dark, locking doors and windows) from the desperate and drastic responses described by the inhabitants of the "war zones" of urban America.

For example, a resident of a high-crime area in St. Louis described for a reporter the three "survival rules" that she and many of her neighbors live by: "Stay off the streets at night unless your life depends on it, keep your children indoors, and never sleep by a window." "We hit the floor," one of her neighbors recounted about a violent incident, when fourteen shots were fired into the house next to hers. "You do that a lot around here." One woman from the same neighborhood hides in her closet when the shooting begins. Another said she would buy a dog for protection were it not for her fear that the dog would be shot. Finally, an elderly woman from this area described the "little traps" for criminals she has set around her home, such as the bucket of water mixed with "something extra" balanced above one of the doors, the strands of "booby-trapped beads" that decorate another doorway, or the lawn mower set strategically at the top of a stairway. These contrivances, motivated by fear, were modeled after those created by a young boy to fend off burglars in the 1990 hit movie *Home Alone*. For this woman, the popular comedy was not a diversion from the rigors of everyday life but a recipe for dealing with them. She saw the film ten times.[44]

American men also tell "war stories" about the extraordinary, if not always effective, precautions they take against crime. A St. Louis man, who required his children to sleep in a bedroom without windows, was preparing to take a bath one evening when gunfire broke out near his house. "As soon as I heard the shooting, I jumped in the tub and lay down in the water," he told a reporter. "It didn't bother me at all that I still had my clothes on. I ruined a good watch." When he heard police sirens, the man ran to the scene of the shooting and found a woman he described as "a good friend" dying on the sidewalk in front of her home.[45] A 78-year-old man from a neighborhood nearby carried all of his money with him whenever he went out, fearing that it would be stolen if left unprotected in his house. He had good reason to be concerned. His home had been burglarized repeatedly, including once while he was in the hospital. On that occasion, all of his plumbing fixtures were taken. One early August morning, on the way to meet a friend for their regular breakfast, he was hit on the head and robbed of $300. He died from the wound a short time later.

The victim's breakfast companion, meanwhile, had several of the windows in his home and in his car broken. He bought a rifle to add to the pistol he already owned for protection. He had used the pistol the previous week to run off some people who were trying to break down his front door. His protection plan was to fight fire with fire: "I'll tell you . . . , they ain't going to run me out. I can get as bad as they can get."[46] The odds do not appear to be in his favor.

Even a courageous man with two guns can only hold out for so long against repeated attacks by forces beyond his control.

Most of these incidents occurred in the early 1990s during a peak in firearm violence in U.S. cities. But even as overall violent crime rates tumbled over the next decade, robberies, assaults, and killings remained common in communities across the country. In November 2003 an eight-year-old boy was fatally wounded by gunfire in the East New York neighborhood of New York City. As one observer commented, "Though devastating in its own right, the murder . . . is just one of many . . . despite assurances by the NYPD, the mayor's office, and the headlines that New York is safer than it's ever been, for everyone." Describing her St. Louis neighborhood in the spring of 2004, a mother of five children observed: "All you hear is 'clack, clack, clack.' People shooting guns." Her friend, a mother of six, described the same sort of protective strategies in use a decade before: "Sometimes you get down on the floor. But you can't get down all the time. You'd be living on the floor."[47]

Life in a War Zone

It has become increasingly common to compare the terror and dangers of living in high-crime areas of America's major cities with those of living under conditions of warfare. A St. Louis woman compared her neighborhood to Bosnia's Sarajevo at the time of the intense ethnic conflict in that country during the early 1990s.[48] Similar comparisons were made between conditions in American cities and the tragic situation in Somalia when U.S. forces were deployed to provide security for agencies providing famine relief. For example, a *Newsweek* columnist asked:

> Why can the United States send forces halfway around the world to disarm Somali drug warlords but not halfway across town to disarm American drug warlords? Why is the government set up so that the national-security advisor each morning gives the President a briefing on world events . . . , but the war at home provokes little more than a few rhetorical expressions of sympathy?[49]

A resident of the South Bronx expressed sympathy for the starving Somalians but was angered by the contrast between the government's response to their plight and the reaction to his own: "It's right that they care and are trying to save lives, but I think that the United States has some gall. If they can't disarm the people in New York with guns, how are they going to go over someplace else and do it?"[50]

More than a decade later, on the opposite coast, Los Angeles Police Chief William Bratton similarly invoked the warfare metaphor to underscore the costs associated with the city's large number of gang killings. These costs include the demands placed on emergency rooms, victim services, prosecutions, and the incarceration of offenders. Bratton called attention to the "peace dividend" that city would reap if gang violence could be brought under control.[51]

The comparisons of the dangers of American cities with those of war are not lost on those American soldiers who must survive in both contexts. A marine who thought he would find Somalia to be exotic and unfamiliar instead discovered conditions there distressingly like those in his neighborhood at home. "The fear of walking the streets without a gun, the fear of someone shooting at you, these are the things I go through every time I go back to D.C."[52] Even U.S. Secretary of Defense Donald Rumsfeld was moved to favorably compare the violence in the streets of Baghdad in the aftermath of the U.S. invasion of Iraq in 2003 with violent crime in Washington, DC: "You've got to remember that if Washington, DC were the size of Baghdad, it would be having something like 215 murders a month. There's going to be violence in a big city." Although Rumsfeld was widely criticized for the comparison, one media observer suggested that his "point about the relative danger of Baghdad and DC is worth examining."[53]

The case of Thanh Tan Le provides a final illustration of the parallels between the warlike conditions in major American cities and those of the battlefield. Le, a former colonel in the South Vietnamese army, emigrated to the United States and was employed as a caseworker for the International Institute of Metropolitan St. Louis, an organization that assists immigrants from Vietnam and other countries in adjusting to the conditions of American life. While on his way to work one morning, he was fatally shot during a carjacking. The local news report on the killing pointed out that Le had survived his country's civil war and eight years in a reeducation camp in Vietnam, "but he couldn't survive the random street violence of American life."[54]

The Struggle for Institutional Control

Warlike conditions not only kill and maim individuals; they also destroy institutions. The relationship works in the opposite direction as well. When local institutions (for example, schools, businesses, families, police forces) are weakened, they lose their capacity to contain crime within manageable bounds. The escalating crime levels that result continue to assault ever more vulnerable institutions, in an ongoing spiral of "disorder and decline." [55]

Local institutions provide order, meaning, purpose, and protection to area residents. Much of the terror surrounding crime is due not simply to the threat of individual victimization but to the sense that the protective cover of institutions has collapsed, exposing individuals to all manner of unpredictable and uncontrollable dangers. Specific institutions perform essential protective functions, often filling in for lapses or weaknesses in the functions of others.

Consider the relationship between the family and the school. In all communities, schools supplement the family by providing essential socialization, support, and supervision for children. In some communities, the schools also offer a refuge from the dangers of the streets. A Chicago 11-year-old wrote in a school essay on violence that he "can't go to school without rolling under cars and dodging bullets."[56] A dozen Philadelphia school children were murdered through March of the 2004 school year, all but one killed away from school grounds.[57] Once in school, however, the shooting is supposed to stop. A chilling illustration of the dependence of children on the protective function of schools in high-risk communities is the response of a student in St. Louis to a killing at her school: "I'm tired of it. You expect this to happen in your own backyard but not in your school."[58]

When the school is invaded by crime, therefore, children may feel doubly threatened: first by the crime itself, and second by the loss of one of the few remaining safe havens left in the community. And the children may not be the only ones who are made fearful. A guidance counselor at a Chicago grade school explains, after the killing of a student:

> There have always been shootings before school and after school. But this happened right at school. It just became more real, more unbearable to everyone. Usually at times like this we just have to deal with the students and the parents. Now we have to deal with the teachers, too. It's just been too much.[59]

A series of highly publicized mass shootings during the 1990s, notable not only for the number of victims they claimed but for the middle-class backgrounds of the offenders and the small-town and suburban locations of the incidents, deeply tarnished the American school's reputation for safety. Between October 1997 and April 1999, in places as distant from high-risk inner-city neighborhoods as Pearl, Mississippi; West Paducah, Kentucky; Jonesboro, Arkansas; Springfield, Oregon; and Littleton, Colorado, middle-class white teenagers killed scores of their classmates, and in some cases their teachers and parents. In the bloodiest of these incidents, at Littleton's Columbine High School, Dylan Klebold and Eric Harris took their own lives after killing 12 of their fellow students and a teacher.[60] The school shootings of the late twentieth century reinforced the violent reputation of the United States, even as overall levels of violent crime were falling, and underscored concerns regarding the deadly connection between widespread firearms availability and homicide. And, ironically perhaps, they provided a basis for consensus between residents of the inner cities and suburbs that there are no safe havens from a rapacious violence one historian has called "the primal problem of American history, the dark reverse of its coin of freedom and abundance."[61]

While the illusion of small-town and suburban invulnerability was dispelled by the school shootings of the 1990s, many inner-city communities suffered utter institutional collapse. A section of the north side of St. Louis, visited by a reporter from New York City during the spring of 2004, provided an example.

> The streets are empty. . . . Row upon row of crumbling storefronts are boarded up. Overgrown ivy spreads across the faces of torched red-brick homes, seemingly strangling the life from them. Tangled weeds grow knee-high across countless vacant lots. Those who live and work here . . . talk about their city by remembering its past. 'That used to be a pretty good bar,' said J.D. Lillard, 64, pointing to a vacant building. . . . 'That was a mechanic shop. That was a big drugstore. That all was a long time ago. They don't cultivate anything. The only thing that grows is crime, and it grows like the weeds.'[62]

A police officer's description of a once-thriving Chicago community reflects the utter institutional barrenness of such areas:

> Do you see any hardware stores? Do you see any grocery stores? Do you see any restaurants? Any bowling alleys? There is nothing here. . . .
> Nothing is worth anything in the area because you open up and you get knocked off, and you get knocked off, and you get knocked off until you give up. . . . In the last few months, three of the last gas stations closed up. The Church's Fried Chicken at Madison and Sacramento finally gave up after being robbed nine days in a row by nine different people. . . . You don't see any newspaper vending machines. Everything we take for granted—a laundromat, a cleaner's, anything. It's not here. The school dropout rate is 70 percent. What do these kids have to do? Nothing.[63]

Not surprisingly, the collapse of community institutions has profound consequences for law enforcement agencies. The task of policing virtual "no-man's-lands" is a daunting one. Under conditions of widespread crime and fear of crime, not only residents begin to view their communities as war zones, as noted earlier, but the police are also prone to develop a warlike mentality that targets average citizens as the enemy. The accompanying hostility and suspicion surrounding police-citizen encounters can lead to tragic consequences.

The case of Amadou Diallo, a young African immigrant who was gunned down by four white police officers as he stood in the doorway of his apartment building in the Bronx, provides a notorious example. The police claimed that they shot in self-defense, fearing that Diallo was reaching for a gun. It turned out that Diallo was unarmed. The object that the police mistook for a gun was his wallet. Despite the fact that the officers fired a total of 41 shots, 19 of which hit their mark, a jury evidently agreed that the police had legitimate grounds to fear for their lives under the circumstances. The officers were acquitted of all charges.[64]

A few years after the Diallo case, another police killing of an innocent black citizen once again shocked the residents of New York City. This time the victim was a 19-year-old high school student named Timothy Stansbury, Jr. Two police officers were patrolling the roofs of buildings in the Louis Armstrong Houses in the Bedford-Stuyvesant housing project. At one of the buildings, one of the officers opened the door leading down the stairs and encountered Stansbury and a few friends, who were planning to take a shortcut to another building via the roof. The officer felt threatened and fired his weapon, killing the unarmed Stansbury. As reported by Police Commissioner Ray Kelly, the shooting happened before anyone could say a word.[65]

How are these scenes of crime, institutional collapse, and community decline to be explained? If, as we have suggested, they are reminiscent of the personal struggles and social destruction of warfare, we must now probe the deeper issues suggested by this analogy. What makes living under conditions of serious crime in the United States so much like living under conditions of war in certain communities? Why are local institutions so vulnerable to collapse? To answer these questions, we must look beyond the local battlegrounds of crime and violence and examine the broader cultural and social context in which local institutions function.

NOTES

1. Adams ([1929] 1969, p. 123).
2. Quoted in Wood (2004).
3. White House News Release (2004).
4. Quoted in Mascaro (2004).
5. This discussion is from Rosenfeld (2004a).
6. The homicide figures are from the FBI's website for the Uniform Crime Reports (http://www.fbi.gov/ucr/01cius.htm) and the Bureau of Justice Statistics' online city homicide data (http://bjsdata.ojp.usdoj.gov/dataonline). Accessed August 15, 2003.
7. Gurr (1989, pp. 45–46). In addition to Gurr, see Shelley (1981) for a classic formulation of the modernization thesis on crime and a review of the historical research on long-term changes in the crime rates of industrial societies.
8. See LaFree (1999), Messner (2003), and Neapolitan (1997) for comprehensive reviews of the cross-national research on crime and economic development.
9. See Neapolitan (1997) and Newman and Howard (1999) for discussions of methodological problems associated with cross-national crime comparisons.
10. Homicide rates are reported for the most recent year available at the time of this writing. The specific years are: U.S. – 2002; Austria and Finland – 2000; Canada and Denmark – 1998; all other nations – 1999. The data for the U.S. were taken from http://www.ojp.usdoj.gov/bjs/glance/tables/hmrttab.htm. The WHO statistics were taken from http://www3.who.int/whosis/mort/.
11. Robbery rates are also reported for the most recent year available at the time of this writing. The robbery rates refer to 2002 for nations other than Canada, Finland, Ireland, Italy, and Sweden. The date for these latter nations is 2001. The Interpol statistics were retrieved online at http://www.interpol.int/Public/Statistics/ICS/.
12. See, for example, van Dijk and Kangaspunta (2000), Lynch (1995, pp. 15–26); Mayhew (1993); Reichel (1994, pp. 28–46).
13. Bayley (1991, pp. 176–177).
14. See Zimring and Hawkins (1997).
15. The data on firearm robberies for England and Wales are for the 12 months ending in March 2000, and were retrieved from www.statistics.gov.uk and www.homeoffice.gov.uk (accessed March 30, 2004). The U.S. data are from the Uniform Crime Reports for calendar year 2000 (www.fbi.gov/ucr), accessed March 30, 2004. The relationship between weapon use in robberies and lethal outcomes is complex. On the one hand, robberies involving guns are less likely to result in an injury because victims are more likely to comply with the robber's demands. On the other hand, victims who have been shot are more likely to die than those who have been injured by other weapons. For discussions of the effects of weapon use on injuries in robberies and violent crimes more generally, see Alba and Messner (1995), Felson and Messner (1996), Kleck (1991), and Kleck and McElrath (1991).
16. The U.S. figure combines inmates held in local jails and state and federal prisons to make it comparable with those of other nations. The incarceration figures are from Harrison and Beck (2003) and Mauer (2003).
17. For discussions of the impact of incarceration on the widely observed "crime drop" in the U.S. during the 1990s, see Conklin (2003) and Spelman (2000).

18. The analogy between criminality and physical illness is advanced by Currie (1999).

19. The data on gun ownership were collected as part of the International Crime Victim Survey, sponsored by the United Nations International Crime Research Institute and the Ministry of Justice of the Netherlands. Richard Block (1998) conducted the analyses referred to in the text.

20. Excellent reviews of research on the relationship between gun ownership and violent crime in the United States can be found in Cook and Moore (1999), Cook, Moore, and Braga (2002), Hemenway (2004), Kleck (1991), and Reiss and Roth (1993).

21. The data on homicide rates and weapon use are from the FBI's *Uniform Crime Reports* for 2002, available online (http://www.fbi.gov/02cius.htm).

22. See Beeghley (2003), Hemenway (2004), and Zimring and Hawkins (1997).

23. Quotations and related material on this incident are from Sanger (1993). A subsequent killing of two Japanese students in Los Angeles during a carjacking aroused a similarly strong reaction among the Japanese public, leading the American ambassador to Japan, Walter Mondale, to go on national television to issue a public apology (see Sanger, 1994).

24. The homicide data in the figure are from National Center for Health Statistics' (NCHS) vital statistics on cause of death based on coroners' and medical examiners' reports. (http://www.ojp.usdoj.gov/bjs/glance/tables/hmrttab.htm). UCR data on homicide go back only to the 1930s. In spite of differences in the way homicides are defined and measured in the vital statistics and UCR data, the two series display a strong correlation over the past 50 years or so (Zahn, 1989, pp. 218–219). See Riedel (1999) for a discussion of the measurement features distinguishing the NCHS and UCR.

25. See Beeghley (2003, p. 61).

26. Archer and Gartner (1984) report homicide time series of varying lengths for many of the nations compared in Figure 2.2. More recent homicide statistics are available from the World Health Organization, as cited above.

27. The data on race differences in homicide victimization risk are from the FBI's *Uniform Crime Reports*, available online (http:www.fbi.gov/ucr/02cius.htm). Anderson and Smith (2003) report statistics on homicide as a cause of death.

28. The race-specific homicide rates are based on counts of race of known offenders in murders published in the *Uniform Crime Reports*, standardized by population figures from the U.S. Bureau of the Census.

29. The first quote is from Keillor (1992); the second is from the testimony of the California savings and loan commissioner before a congressional committee (U.S. Congress House Committee on Government Operations, 1988, p. 34).

30. Sutherland's results are described in his book *White Collar Crime* (1949). The 1980 study is by Clinard and Yeager (1980) and is descrbied by Kappeler, Blumberg, and Potter (1993, p. 111). Rosoff et al. (2003, p. 50) describe the study of the 500 largest corporations.

31. See Rosoff et al. (2003), p. 52.

32. The costs of street crime include economic losses from "property theft or damage, cash losses, medical expenses, and amount of pay lost because of injury or activities related to the crime" (Klaus, 1994, p. 1).

33. Rosoff et al. (2003, pp. 53, 263-268).

34. Rosoff et al. (2003, p. 1).

35. Greenhouse (2004).

36. Consumer Product Safety Commission death and injury figures are from www.cpsc.gov. Data on fatal and nonfatal job-related injuries are from the Bureau of Labor Statistics (www.bls.gov).

37. Kappeler, Blumberg, and Potter (1993, p. 105).

38. Coleman (1994, p. 10).

39. www.osha.gov/oshdoc/toc_fatalfacts.html (accessed April 9, 2004). The case descriptions in the text are from this source.

40. See Barstow (2003a, 2003b); Barstow and Bergman (2003).

41. Barstow (2003b).

42. Barstow (2003b).

43. The cross-national data on protective measures against burglary are taken from the International Crime Victimization Survey, retrieved at: http://www.unicri.it/icvs/publications/pdf_files/key2000i/app4.pdf.

44. These descriptions are from Hernon (1992).

45. Hernon (1992, p. 9A).

46. Bryan (1992).

47. The East New York killing is described in Ince (2003). The descriptions of the St. Louis neighborhood are from Gittrich (2004).

48. Hernon (1992, p. 1A).

49. Alter (1992).

50. Richardson (1992). The *Newsweek* columnist quoted in the text, Jonathan Alter, expressed a similar concern in a later essay, "Why should we settle for peace in the Middle East without peace in the Middle West?" (Alter, 1993).

51. Bratton's remarks are reported in Will (2004).

52. *Newsweek* (1992).

53. Kincaid (2003).

54. Bryan (1996).

55. Skogan (1990) provides an extended discussion of these processes. For a critical appraisal of conventional views about disorder and crime, see Harcourt (2001).

56. Quoted in Terry (1992, p. A6).

57. Caruso (2004).

58. Quoted in Bryan and Little (1993, p. 1A). A rather extreme approach to protecting minority children from such violence has been proposed in a *New York Times* editorial. The columnist draws an analogy between the situation in contemporary American cities and that in London during the blitzkrieg when Britons sent their children out of the city: "What American cities need are evacuation plans to spirit at least some black boys out of harm's way before it's too late" (Staples, 1993).

59. Terry (1992). For an account of a teacher's effort to protect a student from an armed attack by a gang in a St. Louis classroom, see Little (1994).

60. *Newsweek* (1999); Gibbs (1999).

61. The historian David Courtwright was quoted in Patterson (1999).

62. Gittrich (2004)

63. Quoted in Soll (1993, p. 57).

64. For details about the Diallo case, see *Time Daily* (2000) and *Time Magazine* (2000).

65. Details about the Stansbury killing can be found in Parascandola and Perez (2004) and McPhee, McQuillan, and Goldiner (2004). Cases of fatal errors in police perceptions of citizen-threat are not limited to New York City. As Wills (2000, p. A7) reports, in Illinois "a man was shot by the police because he had a fork, and a woman was shot because she was holding a cell phone."

3

Ships in the Night

Theoretical Perspectives in Contemporary Criminology

Ships that pass in the night, and speak each other in passing,
Only a signal shown and a distant voice in the darkness;
So on the ocean of life, we pass and speak one another,
Only a look and a voice, then darkness again and a silence.
HENRY WADSWORTH LONGFELLOW, "THE THEOLOGIAN'S
TALE: ELIZABETH"

James F. Short, Jr., past president of both the American Society of Criminology and the American Sociological Association, has called attention to a problem pervasive in scholarly debates as well as in everyday discourse. Very often spirited exchanges seem to go nowhere because the participants fail to recognize that they are not really talking about the same thing. Like ships that pass in the night, the verbal combatants talk past one another.[1] Not surprisingly, such debates generate more heat than light on the topic under consideration.

In this chapter, we try to forestall this kind of miscommunication—first, by clearly delimiting the *scope conditions* of our explanation of the American crime problem and, second, by making explicit the set of concepts and assumptions underlying our approach, that is, by making explicit our analytic paradigm.[2] The scope conditions of an explanation specify the limits within which its claims are assumed to hold. Our explanation of the American crime problem has two key scope conditions. One concerns the level of explanation, and the other involves the seriousness of the crimes to which the explanation applies. We seek to explain *macrolevel* differences (that is, differences across groups or populations) in rates of the most serious types of crime. Our analysis is not directly concerned with the *individual-level* question of why some persons are more or less likely than others to commit criminal acts; nor does our explanation encompass the types of crimes that are generally regarded by the public, policy makers, and criminologists alike as less serious than the forms of criminal violence and very serious economic crimes addressed in Chapter 2.

By contrast, the major theoretical perspectives on crime and delinquency orient themselves to the individual level of analysis and, while not precluding serious crimes, have tended to focus on less serious forms of offending. Their scope conditions, in other words, diverge from those guiding our explanation of crime. Theories with different scope conditions cannot be compared directly because they seek to explain different phenomena. It is possible, however, to link these individual-level theories of crime with macrolevel explanations that share a similar causal logic. We can then evaluate these macrolevel explanations in terms of their ability to explain variation in the rates of serious crimes.

In the second part of this chapter, we introduce the sociological paradigm informing our analysis and argue that the failure of major theoretical perspectives within contemporary criminology to offer a satisfactory explanation of macro-level variation in crimes results from either a distorted or underdeveloped use of this analytical framework. Our review encompasses the major individual-level perspectives in sociological criminology—social learning, control, and strain—and their macrolevel analogues—cultural deviance, social disorganization, and anomie. Among the existing perspectives, anomie theory comes closest, in our view, to providing a convincing account of the American crime problem. However, anomie theory also requires considerable clarification and expansion to fully realize its explanatory potential. In Chapter 4, we present a sociological explanation of crime based on a revised version of anomie theory that is capable of accounting for the comparatively high rates of serious crime in the United States.

THE SCOPE CONDITIONS OF CONTEMPORARY CRIMINOLOGICAL THEORIES

Levels of Explanation

One of the primary reasons for miscommunication in debates about crime is confusion over levels of explanation.[3] Much of the inquiry into crime, by professional criminologists and laypersons alike, occurs at the individual level of analysis. The basic question underlying the individualistic approach, as noted earlier, is why one person rather than another commits a criminal act. The answer to this type of question must encompass attributes or predispositions of individuals, including biological traits, psychological states, and personal socialization experiences.

In contrast, analysis at the macrolevel focuses on questions about groups and populations. The relevant questions here include the following: Why do levels of crime vary across social systems (for example, nations, cities, neighborhoods)? Why is crime patterned in systematic ways across social categories within a social system (for instance, by race, class, age, gender)? Macrolevel questions are framed in terms of rates of crime, by adding up all of the individual acts of crime recorded in a particular area or ostensibly committed by (or against) members of a specified group or category. In practice, the complexity of the construction of crime rates reflects the decisions and behaviors of those reporting victimizations and those recording these incidents. Crime rates ultimately reflect not merely the level of some kind of behavior but the "criminalization" of that behavior as well.[4] Nevertheless, the rate itself does not really describe any given individual. Rather, the crime rate is a property of a human aggregate. Émile Durkheim referred to such properties as "social facts" and argued convincingly that social facts are best explained by other social facts. In other words, the most appropriate explanations of the questions about crime rates—unlike questions about individual acts of crime— refer to other properties of collective units.[5]

The distinction between individual- and macrolevel explanations is important because neither can be fully reduced to the other. To illustrate, consider the phenomenon of unemployment. A plausible explanation for why one person rather than another loses his or her job might be formulated in terms of education. Evidence indicates that the risk of unemployment decreases along with the attainment of higher levels of education. In General Social Surveys conducted between the early 1970s and the early 2000s, for example, respondents with a college education were only about half as likely as those with just a high school degree to be unemployed. Respondents who had not completed high school, in turn, were more than twice as likely to be out of work than respondents who had completed high school. The bar graph displayed in Figure 3.1 shows this relationship between education and unemployment at the individual level.[6]

The relationship between aggregate educational characteristics of the U.S. population and the rate of unemployment, however, does not reflect the strong relationship between individual educational attainment and unemployment risk. As shown in Figure 3.2, the relative size of the college-educated population climbed steadily over recent decades, increasing from 7.7 percent in 1960, to 16.2 percent in 1980, to just over 25 percent at the turn of the century. On the basis of the individual-level relationship between education and unemployment, then, one might expect that the nation's unemployment rate would have declined steadily as a result of the substantial growth of the college-educated population during this period. Yet unemployment rates (the percent of the civilian labor force unemployed) have fluctuated since the 1960s, rising and falling along with

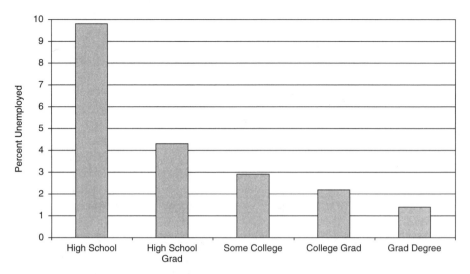

FIGURE 3.1 The Relationship Between Unemployment and Educational Attainment, 1972–2002 (Individual Level)

recessions and economic expansions. In general, little relationship appears to exist between unemployment and educational attainment at the macrolevel of analysis. For the years shown in Figure 3.2, the correlation between the two series is a very modest –0.17 and not statistically significant.[7]

Given the individual-level relationship between educational level and unemployment in the United States, we also might expect that, if we looked across nations, those with higher rates of educational attainment would have lower rates of unemployment. But this turns out not to be the case. Figure 3.3 displays a scatterplot of the unemployment rate and university enrollment per 1,000 population for 25 European nations during the early 1990s.[8] Each symbol represents a given nation's values on the two measures, as illustrated in the figure for the country of Ireland. Ireland had an enrollment rate of 33 university students per 1,000 population and an unemployment rate of 12 percent. If we were to draw straight lines from those values on the respective axes of the figure, Ireland lies at the intersection of the two lines. The location of each of the nations in the scatterplot is determined in this way.

A perfect positive relationship between unemployment and education would be indicated by all the points forming a straight line running from the bottom left to the top right corner of the scatterplot. For each unit increase in education, in other words, we would observe a corresponding increase in unemployment. Likewise, a perfect negative relationship would be indicated by all the points forming a line from the top left to the bottom right corner of the scatterplot, meaning that for every unit increase in education there would be a corresponding decrease in unemployment. What we actually see in Figure 3.3 looks nothing like either of these scenarios. The points representing each country's joint values on the unemployment and education measures exhibit little systematic pattern; they

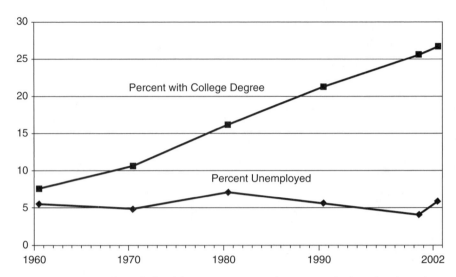

FIGURE 3.2 The Relationship Between Unemployment and Educational Attainment, 1960–2002 (Macrolevel)

really are "scattered" around the figure. Little or no relationship exists between unemployment and education for this sample of European countries. In fact, the correlation between the two variables is small ($r = 0.20$) and not significantly different from zero.

Therefore, the strong relationship between schooling and unemployment that we observe for individuals is not reproduced at the macrolevel, whether we look across nations or over time in the United States. That does not mean unemployment and education are unrelated, but that the strength, direction, and meaning of their relationship differ across the two levels of analysis. "Macroeconomic" explanations for the rate of unemployment often use concepts that are not directly applicable to individual-level analysis because they do not describe properties of persons. The precise causes of unemployment levels are not fully understood, but many economists point to factors such as interest rates, inflation, governmental transfer programs (unemployment insurance, food stamps), tax policies, and international trade deficits. No strict counterparts exist at the individual level for these macrolevel concepts. As a result, explanations of unemployment rates that employ such concepts will necessarily differ from individual-level explanations.

Hodgins's criminological research on the impact of mental disorder and intellectual deficiency on criminal behavior in a Swedish birth cohort explicitly recognizes the distinction between levels of explanation. The study found persons with mental disorders and intellectual deficits significantly more likely than others to commit both property and violent crimes. However, Hodgins cautions against generalizing these individual-level findings to the macrolevel. For example, the results cannot account for differences in crime rates between the United States and Sweden, because levels of mental disorder and intellectual deficiency are

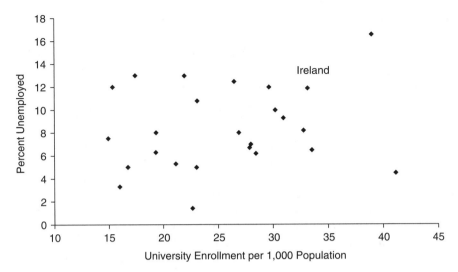

FIGURE 3.3 The Relationship between Unemployment and Educational Attainment in 25 European Nations

about the same in the two nations. Moreover, given the high rates of crime in the United States, "the crimes of those with major psychiatric disorders and intellectual handicaps seem insignificant in comparison."[9]

We do not mean to suggest that individual-level inquiry is unimportant; it obviously is indispensable for a comprehensive understanding of crime. Any macrolevel explanation of crime will inevitably be predicated on underlying premises about individual behavior.[10] We simply want to emphasize that our objectives in this book are distinctly macrolevel in character. Indeed, because the questions that we ask are questions about aggregate patterns of crime, we employ an explanatory framework built around basic properties of social organization. We rely on one set of social facts—features of social organization such as culture and social structure—to explain another set of social facts—American crime rates compared with those of other developed nations.

Serious Crimes

In addition to limiting our focus to macrolevel questions, we also restrict the scope of the analysis to a specific domain of criminal behavior, namely, serious crimes. By this we mean violations of criminal law involving significant bodily injury, the threat of bodily injury, or, in the case of nonviolent offenses, significant economic harm to victims, both individual and collective. What distinguishes significant from non-significant threats and harms is inherently arbitrary. Consequently, it is best to think of crimes as arrayed on a continuum, from the most serious at one end to the least serious at the other.[11] The evidence and arguments that we present, with few exceptions, restrict themselves in application and scope to the serious end of the continuum.

It might seem self-evident that criminologists should devote most of their attention to crimes that nearly everyone regards as serious. However, much criminological research over the past several decades has been devoted to the study of relatively minor criminal infractions. Professional disagreements over what types of crime to class as most serious do not explain the relative neglect of serious offending by contemporary criminologists. Few criminologists would dispute the claim that homicide and robbery, for example, are serious crimes. Methodology forms part of the reason that criminologists have not paid more attention to such offenses. Serious offending, engaged in by small numbers of people, is difficult to study via the survey research methods that have been favored by recent generations of researchers. Prohibitively large samples would have to be drawn from the general population to secure a sufficient number of street criminals or corporate criminals for reliable analysis, even assuming such persons would tell the truth about their illegal activities. Yet there are other ways of obtaining information from people who commit serious crimes (for example, they can be interviewed in prison), and, ideally, the choice of research issues should not be driven by methodological considerations.[12]

Another possible reason for the relative neglect of serious crimes in contemporary criminology is more substantive in nature. It might be argued that serious crimes do not warrant extensive attention precisely because they are so infrequent. In other words, because serious crimes affect fewer people than nonserious crimes, the aggregate (if not individual) harm associated with serious crimes might be regarded as less than that of nonserious crimes, thereby rendering the former less important for analytical purposes. However, this line of reasoning understates the frequency and impact of serious offending, especially in the category of white-collar crime. In addition, a full appreciation of the practical importance of serious crimes requires an assessment of both their frequency relative to less serious crimes and their frequency relative to other behaviors or conditions that result in significant harm (such as automobile accidents and infectious disease). Interpersonal violence is now recognized as a public health problem as well as a law enforcement problem in the United States because, in the words of two public health researchers, it "exacts such a high toll in illness, death and quality of life."[13]

Homicide is the second leading cause of death for men between the ages of 15 and 24 in the United States, and the third leading cause of death for those between 25 and 34 years old. Assault is the sixth leading cause of nonfatal injury among men between 15 and 44. Criminal violence takes a particularly tragic toll on African-Americans. Homicide is the leading cause of death among black males, ages 15 to 34. Among 15–24-year-old black women, homicide is the second leading cause of death (after unintentional injury); for those between 25 and 34, homicide ranks fifth. Even acknowledging that these comparisons reflect declines in other causes of injury and death, as well as decreasing risk from criminal violence during the 1990s, it can hardly be said that serious crime is a rare cause of death or physical injury in the United States.[14]

Finally, it has been argued that, regardless of their frequency or effects, serious crimes do not require special explanation; they can be explained by the same perspectives that are applied to less serious crimes. Two criminologists have presented an influential "general" theory of crime (that is, a theory with very broad scope conditions) that does not distinguish between more serious and less serious forms of criminality.[15] The empirical foundation for our analysis, however, lies in the evidence of comparatively high levels of serious crime in the United States, as reported in the previous chapter. We are uncertain about whether the United States would exhibit distinctively high levels of offending for minor offenses. In fact, it seems plausible that relatively minor legal violations are commonplace throughout the modern world and that appreciable differences among nations are likely to emerge only for criminal behaviors closer to the serious pole of the crime continuum. A United Nations study of cross-national crime patterns lends support to this position. Comparing crime patterns in the United States with those in other countries, the researchers conclude that "conventional crime and corruption in the United States are not exceptionally high. The most important difference appears to be the high level of homicides and robberies, which in the United States often involve guns."[16] We thus prefer to leave open the possibility that explanations of serious crimes may differ in important respects from explanations of other crimes, and we restrict the scope conditions of our arguments accordingly.

The explanation of crime that we offer differs, then, in important respects from those that currently dominate criminological thinking. At the same time, however, our analysis of the American crime problem draws heavily from existing perspectives. We do not reject contemporary explanations of crime; rather, we seek to recast them in a broad macrosociological conceptual framework capable of accounting for variations across societies in rates of serious crime.

THE UNFULFILLED PROMISE OF THE
SOCIOLOGICAL PARADIGM

A basic axiom of sociological analysis is that human behavior can be understood as a product of social organization. The two basic dimensions of social organization are culture and social structure. In sociological usage, culture refers to values, beliefs, goals, and norms—the entire "symbolic-meaningful" level of human action. Social structure consists of the patterned relationships among persons and groups defined and organized through social institutions.[17] The basic concepts of culture and social structure, and assumptions about their interrelationships, give rise to the sociological paradigm. In this book, we apply the general sociological paradigm to the specific social phenomenon of crime.

The major theoretical perspectives in contemporary criminology usually are described as sociological, but they are in fact more accurately viewed as social-psychological in orientation. Social learning theory, for example, emphasizes the ways in which individuals acquire beliefs, attitudes, and behavior patterns conducive to crime. Social control theory posits that criminal behavior results when the individual's bonds to others are weakened. Strain theory proposes that criminality results from negative experiences, especially goal frustration associated with the discrepancy between an individual's aspirations, on the one hand, and achievements or expectations, on the other.

Although these perspectives have been formulated in individualistic terms, they can be related to companion macrolevel theories, which have a more distinctly sociological cast. Social learning theories are associated with cultural deviance theories, which explain crime as the product of cultural or subcultural values and norms. Social control theory is most closely connected with social disorganization theory at the macrolevel of analysis. Social disorganization refers to the inability of groups or communities to realize collective goals, including the goal of crime control. Finally, strain theory is commonly linked with anomie theory. In its most general formulation, anomie refers to a weakening in the normative regulation of behavior. Anomie theory posits that social norms begin to lose their regulatory force when people are unable to realize their cultural goals by using the institutionally approved means.

The macrolevel criminological perspectives are most directly relevant to our analysis because they share the same scope conditions. However, the explanations of crime associated with these perspectives commonly contain references to individual behavior. In this sense, the macrolevel perspectives themselves are not consistently or exclusively sociological. It is most useful, then, to think of dominant criminological approaches as "hybrid" theories—cultural-social learning, disorganization-control, and anomie-strain—that actually combine individual- and macrolevel concepts and empirical referents.

The relationship between macrolevel theory and individual-level processes is actually quite complex and the subject of considerable debate among criminologists. For example, although the anomie perspective is most commonly linked with strain theory at the individual level, several criminologists have argued that a "control" model of individual behavior is also compatible with the logic of anomie theory.[18] We follow the conventional practice of joining strain theory and anomie theory in our review of existing criminological theories. As will become clear in Chapter 4, our proposed macrolevel explanation of crime incorporates elements from each of the three major hybrid perspectives on crime.

In addition to the cultural-social learning, disorganization-control, and anomie-strain perspectives, two other major theoretical perspectives are often considered sociological: the labeling (or societal reaction) perspective and the conflict perspective. Labeling theory makes its principal contribution by calling attention to the interplay between social control and personal identity. Labeling theorists specify the processes through which efforts at crime control contribute to the stabilization of criminal roles and self-images. Conflict theories emphasize the political nature of crime production, posing the questions of how the norms of particular groups are encoded into law and how, in turn, law is used as a means by which certain groups dominate others.

Both these perspectives contain important insights about the creation and enforcement of rules in a society, but neither perspective focuses primarily on the causes of the behavior that is subject to labeling or criminalization by political authorities. We orient our inquiry toward questions about the causes of variation in rates of criminal behavior, and accordingly we focus our attention on those theoretical perspectives that address such questions directly: the "etiological" perspectives on crime.[19]

In the discussion that follows, we seek to place the major etiological perspectives within a broad sociological framework. Each of the perspectives is associated with a dimension of social organization. Cultural-social learning explanations emphasize how crime varies with the strength of criminal subcultures. Disorganization-control explanations emphasize the structural dimension, specifically, how crime rates vary with the strength of social relationships and social controls. Finally, anomie-strain theory unites the two dimensions of social organization in its explanation of crime. Although each perspective offers a unique contribution to an explanation of crime at the macrolevel, each is also limited in important respects. We intend our analysis to build on the strengths of the alternative perspectives and, at the same time, to overcome their limitations by joining them in a single, unifying paradigm.

Cultural-Social Learning Explanations of Crime

"A person becomes delinquent," Edwin Sutherland writes, "because of an excess of definitions favorable to violation of law over definitions unfavorable to violation of law."[20] Sutherland's principle of differential association lies at the center of cultural and subcultural explanations of crime. Criminal behavior is learned behavior, Sutherland insists, and it is learned under the same conditions and in the same ways conforming behavior is learned—in association with like-minded others. Social reinforcement and cultural validation are required whether one is learning to become a butcher or a dentist, a burglar or a rapist.

This normalizing focus is a source of the tremendous appeal and genuine importance of Sutherland's formulation. Criminal behavior is normal in the sense that it requires socially learned motivations and socially structured supports. Crime is normal, in a word, because it is social, and it is no less social than conformity. However, Sutherland's idea and, by implication, all cultural explanations of crime go further. Crime not only arises from the same social sources as conformity; crime *is* conformity. Cultural explanations of deviance assume that people violate the normative standards of groups to which they do not belong by conforming to the standards of the groups to which they do belong. Thorsten Sellin introduced into the literature the famous example of the Sicilian father who expresses surprise at his arrest by New Jersey authorities for killing the seducer of his teenage daughter. He was, after all, only doing what he had to do to uphold the conduct codes of "the old country."[21]

We may derive the following general proposition from accounts such as this one: Conformity to the standards of group or subgroup A causes deviation from the standards of group or subgroup B. People violate the standards of groups to which they do not belong. As a corollary, they do not, at least in the theoretically interesting case, violate the standards of the groups to which they do belong. Critics have responded to these propositions from cultural deviance theory by arguing, reasonably enough, that the theory has no answer to the question of why someone might violate his or her own rules.[22]

Actually, the theory does have an answer for this question; however, the answer, found in the idea of culture conflict, supports the critics' general point. In all societies, people belong to many social groups, not just one. In highly complex urban industrial societies, in particular, these multiple group memberships may expose people to conflicting behavioral standards. To conform to one is, ipso facto, to violate another. This idea of crime as produced by culture conflict still remains rooted in a theory of crime-as-conformity. In culture-conflict explanations, just as in cultural explanations of crime more generally, deviance remains but the residual consequence of conformity. Without conformity, there is no (cultural) deviance.

In an important sense, then, cultural "deviance" theories are not theories of deviance at all. This is their distinctive strength, and it is their major shortcoming as an explanation of crime and other forms of deviance. Again, the strength of the cultural-social learning perspective is that it calls attention to the normal character of much deviant behavior. It provides a purely social (or social-psychological) explanation of behavior and does not rely on or imply underlying psychological abnormality. It highlights the irony of deviance by showing how the extraordinary results from the ordinary, how the very conspiracy of the normal—the intensity and effectiveness of a group's efforts to promote conformity to its norms—produces the abnormal. The explanation of crime that we develop in this book is heavily indebted to this insight.

However, the idea that criminal behavior is learned (at the individual level) and that crime is entirely the product of culture (at the macrolevel) quickly runs into several interrelated problems. The perspective risks the danger of circular reasoning. If one assumes that all behavior is consistent with underlying values, then criminal acts themselves must be regarded as evidence of the presence of criminal values. The theory then becomes nonfalsifiable: Criminal acts will always be associated with criminal values. Any effort to restrict the scope conditions of the perspective to only certain kinds of crime ultimately leads to the same problem. Cultural theories, then, explain those crimes for which there is cultural support; in other words, the theory explains those crimes that it is capable of explaining!

The adoption of an overly broad conception of culture also encourages circular reasoning. Ruth Kornhauser identifies the omnibus definition of culture as the central analytical deficiency in the cultural approach to deviance. She writes:

> When everything is included under the rubric of culture, nothing is
> left with which to compare the causal importance of culture.
> How can such theories be tested? If culture includes all learned
> behavior irrespective of whether it is directed toward the realization
> of cultural values, then culture will always be the sole cause of
> behavior. If culture includes social organization, then the constraints
> imposed by the patterning of social relationships will simply be
> viewed as culturally determined.[23]

Finally, the cultural perspective runs the risk of trivialization. An explanation of crime that simply describes cultural differences between criminals and non-criminals remains inherently unsatisfying. Ernest van den Haag has summarized the problem concisely: "Surely crime is largely produced by the life styles generated by the subcultures characteristic of those who commit it. But does this tell us more than that crime is produced by a crime-producing subculture?"[24]

What produces the crime-producing subculture? Where do "definitions favorable to law violation" or "reinforcements for deviant behavior" come from? If criminal behavior is the product of socialization into the conduct codes of deviant subcultures, then to avoid trivialization and circularity, the cultural explanation of crime must account for the emergence, prevalence, content, and strength of deviant subcultures. This is difficult to do without recourse to the other dimension of social organization—social structure.[25]

Disorganization-Control Explanations of Crime

Disorganization-control explanations focus precisely on the structural dimension of social organization. Theorists in this camp maintain that criminality is the consequence not of culture but of the absence of culture. From the disorganization-control perspective, there is no need to account for a culturally induced "motivation" to break the rules. Driven by strong biological urges and pure self-interest, human beings are naturally predisposed to deviate. The basic question posed by control theory is not why some people break the rules but, rather, why the rest of us do not.[26]

The answer to this question is that most people obey the rules because they are restrained by social controls. Those who become criminal are thus those who lack such controls. Or, in Travis Hirschi's more elaborate formulation, people deviate from conventional rules of conduct because the bonds that attach them to others, commit them to conventional lines of action, involve them in conventional activities, and sustain their belief in the cultural standards themselves weaken or break.

Control theory is often faulted for begging the question of why bonds weaken or fail to develop in the first place. However, its macrolevel analogue—social disorganization theory—offers a partial answer to this question. Sociologists at the University of Chicago developed social disorganization theory in the early twentieth century. The work of the Chicago School sociologists has inspired a tradition of inquiry into the social-ecological organization of the city. The resulting orientation to the spatial patterning of behavior in urban areas has given rise, in turn, to what has been aptly termed "neighborhood criminology."

The classic neighborhood criminologists were Clifford R. Shaw and Henry D. McKay, who applied the basic principles of the Chicago School to explain neighborhood crime rates.[27] Neighborhoods with the highest crime rates are those, Shaw and McKay argued, with high levels of residential instability, ethnic heterogeneity, and, most important, economic deprivation. These conditions erode the capacity of local institutions—businesses, schools, churches, families—to impose controls over the behavior of residents, especially children and adolescents. Moreover, weakened neighborhoods are unable to withstand or control "invasions" of new residents, who may bring with them distinct cultural traditions that impede communication and cooperation with older inhabitants. Even in the absence of cultural differences, the continuous arrival of new people (and the departure of former inhabitants) makes it difficult to maintain the kin and friendship networks, and the more formal associations, necessary for effective crime control. Shaw and McKay used the term "social disorganization" to describe the inability of a neighborhood to manage its boundaries, ward off invasion, and prevent delinquency and crime—in short, to "control itself." Their theory of social disorganization and neighborhood social control has undergone important changes over the last half-century or so. Yet the basic idea that crime rates vary with a community's capacity to control the behavior of its members remains intact.[28]

The essential contribution of the disorganization-control perspective to a sociological explanation of crime is that it can answer the question that is not addressed adequately by learning theory and cultural deviance theory, namely, why people violate rules of the groups to which they belong. Moreover, control and social disorganization theorists justly criticize cultural deviance theorists for overemphasizing cultural support for crime and underemphasizing the lack of structural support for conformity. Yet, in spite of the fact that they are conceptual opposites, or perhaps because of it, disorganization-control theorists end up committing the same type of analytical error committed by cultural-social learning theorists: They expunge from the explanatory framework one of the two fundamental features of social organization, in this case, culture.

Disorganization-control theorists and researchers have gone to great lengths over the years to expel culture from the causes of crime. The crusade against culture stems in part from the understandable desire to avoid association with the "pathological" tradition in the study of American social problems, which tended to equate disorganization with deviation from small-town, Protestant, middle-class standards.[29] Also, as pointed out earlier, there are very real problems associated with the "pure" cultural explanations of crime and deviance, such as the overly broad conception of culture. Yet the response of disorganization-control theorists has been to propose an equally broad conception of "structure."

The work of Ruth Kornhauser, whose criticisms of the cultural approach have already been noted, provides an apt illustration. As a corrective to an overly expansive concept of culture, Kornhauser proposes restricting the realm of culture to the "ultimate" ends and meanings of existence. Not all values, she insists, are cultural values, and not all symbolic meanings are located in culture. Cultural values specify the end points, not the instrumental means, of human action; cultural symbols are those, and only those, "richly elaborated in their meaning for the self."[30]

Kornhauser's restrictive definition of culture makes cultural explanation of any kind nearly impossible. How much social behavior, conforming or deviant, that occurs with any frequency is, after all, directly anchored to the end points of existence? The difficulty with her conception of culture is a mirror image of the conceptual problem she so deftly analyzes in cultural deviance theory. If cultural theorists amplify culture, packing it so full of meaning that it loses any distinctive analytical usefulness, then Kornhauser similarly distorts the concept of social structure. The question must be asked, if not all values are cultural values—indeed, if most are not—then what else could they be? Kornhauser's answer is the only one possible: They are "structural values."[31]

Kornhauser's notion of structural values has two fundamental problems. First, her expansive view of structure makes it virtually impossible in practice to assess the importance of structural factors relative to cultural ones. This is exactly analogous to the problem associated with cultural theories recognized by Kornhauser herself. Hardly anything is "left out" of structure with which structural variables could be compared.

Second, the concept of structural values, if taken literally, undermines the essential distinction between the two components of social organization. The meanings of culture and social structure must be kept unambiguously distinct precisely because they are empirically inseparable. Culture and social structure are not "things" that can be neatly separated. They are analytical constructs that call attention to different aspects of the same underlying social phenomena. They are different ways of perceiving and understanding the nature of social reality and the causes of social behavior. They are, in brief, points of view for analyzing the social world.

Kornhauser acknowledges the importance of making an analytical distinction between the two dimensions of social organization. She applauds a classic statement by Kroeber and Parsons that sought to end, or at least to clarify, the dispute between anthropologists and sociologists concerning the relative significance of culture and social structure.[32] Yet her treatment of social organization runs counter to their instruction. For Kroeber and Parsons, there could be no such thing as a "structural value." Their point in setting forth an explicit distinction between the two dimensions of social organization was to prevent this kind of absorption of one by the other. Social structure should be limited in scope to the "relational" or interactional component of social systems. Culture should be limited to the dimension of value, belief, and knowledge. To blur this distinction, in their view and ours, destroys the analytical usefulness of both concepts.

The Common Origins of Cultural Deviance Theory and Social Disorganization Theory

Remembering that the concepts of culture and social structure, like all concepts, are analytical tools helps make sense of an otherwise very puzzling aspect of the history of sociological studies of crime in America. Both cultural deviance theory and its putative rival, social disorganization theory, were developed at essentially the same time, in the same place, by many of the same people, and in response to the same social reality: the early twentieth-century urban slum.

The connection between the preeminent cultural theory, Sutherland's theory of differential association, and Shaw and McKay's theory of social disorganization is particularly noteworthy. Differential association theory was originally conceived within a broader conceptual framework that attributed crime to both cultural conflict and structural disorganization. In an early formulation of his theory, Sutherland notes that what he termed "systematic" (that is, patterned and continuous) criminal behavior "is due immediately to differential association in a situation in which cultural conflicts exist, and ultimately to the social disorganization in that situation."[33]

After World War II, Sutherland broke with the social disorganization tradition in the sociology of crime. He explicitly rejected the very idea of social disorganization in favor of the concept of differential social organization. According to this view, crime rates tend to be higher in poor urban areas not because these areas lack social order but because they are apt to contain multiple subcultures, some of which are organized around "definitions favorable to law violation." The subgroups that carry such definitions are no less "organized" for promoting criminal rather than conforming behavior.[34]

Sutherland's break with disorganization theory did not occur because the urban social world that he observed differed from the one observed by the disorganization theorists. Again, the difference between the cultural deviance and social disorganization perspectives is more conceptual than empirical. The difference is fundamentally a matter of which elements of social reality an observer chooses to "see" and considers theoretically important. Because all groups of any complexity will contain some normative patterns that conflict with the law and some social structures that are too weak to sustain conformity to law, it is not surprising that social disorganization theorists could identify the degree of disorganization in a group as a relevant factor for explaining crime, while cultural theorists could focus on group (or subgroup) support for crime.

We know that the differences between cultural deviance and social disorganization researchers that originally emerged within the Chicago School are not primarily due to differences in the empirical phenomena that they observed, because both sides claim the same observers—Shaw and McKay—to be in their own camp. And both sides are correct. Shaw and McKay held that social disorganization in an urban area produces delinquency, directly by weakening community controls, and indirectly by generating a subculture of delinquent "traditions" passed on over time by one generation of delinquents to another. Once it emerges, the delinquent subculture attains a life of its own, and it in fact becomes part of the organization of some lower-class communities. Shaw and McKay's explanation of crime is based, therefore, on a mixed model of community social organization, combining key elements of both social disorganization theory (for example, weak ties to conventional institutions) and cultural deviance theory (for instance, socialization into delinquent codes).[35]

Explanations of crime based on mixed models are not universally popular in contemporary criminology. Control theorists have a particularly strong disdain for them.[36] For example, Kornhauser describes Shaw and McKay's disorganization-subcultural explanation of delinquency as "untenable," maintaining that it produced a "confusion between cause and effect that plagues delinquency theory to this day." She concludes that Shaw and McKay's model is not only mixed but contradictory: Its social disorganization assumptions cannot be true if its cultural deviance assumptions are also true.[37] Even if Kornhauser's assessment of Shaw and McKay's explanation is correct, however, it would not necessarily invalidate other explanations of crime based on such mixed models.

In any case, our point in reviewing the common theoretical origins of cultural deviance theory and social disorganization theory is to suggest that any explanation of crime that fully exploits the sociological paradigm will be, to one degree or another, a mixed-model explanation because the sociological paradigm is itself a mixed model. It relates crime to social organization, which encompasses both culture and social structure. Far from viewing this as a shortcoming, we think that criminological explanation can only benefit from an analytical framework that calls attention to both aspects of social reality. The third major perspective in criminology—anomie-strain theory—has the virtue of applying the sociological paradigm in its totality rather than in the fractured form characteristic of other contemporary approaches.

Anomie-Strain Explanations of Crime

Anomie theory is capable of answering the questions about the causes of crime left open or defined away by the cultural-social learning and disorganization-control perspectives. These perspectives are deficient, we have argued, because they exaggerate the causal importance of one of the dimensions of social organization—structure in the case of disorganization theory and culture in the case of cultural theory—and downplay the importance of the other dimension. By contrast, anomie theory incorporates both dimensions in an explanation that, whatever its empirical failings, has the great advantage of being conceptually complete.

Robert Merton presented the classic formulation of anomie theory in his 1938 essay "Social Structure and Anomie." He clarified and expanded, but did not fundamentally alter, his thesis in papers published over the succeeding several decades.[38] When cast in the terms of the sociological paradigm described earlier, Merton's theory attributes crime to the lack of articulation within and between the basic components of social organization: culture and social structure. Merton subdivides culture (what he refers to as the "culture structure") into two parts: (1) the society's central value and goal orientations, or ends, and (2) the institutionalized means for attaining them. The social structure, in Merton's formulation, distributes access to the legitimate means for attaining highly valued goals. Crime and deviance result, then, from the malintegration of elements within culture and from a similar lack of fit between culture and social structure.

In the first case, excessive cultural emphasis is placed on success goals, and correspondingly less emphasis is placed on the legitimate means for achieving the goals. In sociological terms, success goals are strongly institutionalized. They are widely and deeply internalized in the population and are accompanied by sharply etched images of successful persons or roles (for example, the "village elders" in some societies and "captains of industry" in others). Simply put, they are the goals that "everyone" knows about, that "everyone" thinks are important, and that "everyone" strives for. By contrast, the legitimate means to attain the goals are neither as well-defined in society nor as salient to personal or collective action. Because they are not as strongly institutionalized, they lack the overwhelmingly and universally obligatory character of success goals. Considerable discretion is allowed in one's orientation to means, which implies greater tolerance for deviance from means than from goals. The greater the emphasis on goals relative to means, then, the stronger the pressure on persons to deviate from established modes of behavior, including legal standards, in the pursuit of culturally defined success.

The second way in which social organization produces crime, according to Merton, is by unequally distributing opportunities to achieve success goals in the population. Because of their privileged position in the social structure, by which Merton means primarily the class system, some persons or groups have advantages over others in the pursuit of success. Yet all are striving for the same goals. Social structure in this sense contradicts culture. Culture promises what social structure cannot deliver—success, for all. People faced with this contradiction between cultural mandate and structural impediment are subject to pressures or "strain" to abandon legal but ineffective means of goal attainment in favor of illegal, effective ones. These pressures are particularly acute, Merton argues, for members of the lower class, who lack access to the legitimate means of attaining the goals shared by members of all classes.

Both dimensions of social organization are thus fully implicated in Merton's explanation of crime. Unlike control theory, anomie theory emphasizes the importance of culture in the generation of crime and deviance. Unlike cultural-social learning theory, however, anomie theory does not assume that deviance is simply a matter of cultural definition or differential socialization. Anomie theory does not require the existence of deviant culture to explain deviant behavior. On the contrary, Merton proposes that criminal behavior results, in part, from conformity to conventional standards of success—but only in part. The great analytical advantage of anomie theory over alternative perspectives on crime is that it always calls attention back to the cultural and structural contexts of conformity to or deviation from conventional goals and means. Crime results when conformity to conventional success goals occurs in the context of a cultural overemphasis on ends relative to means and in the context of structural inequality of access to the approved means. Neither cultural conformity nor structural deprivation is, by itself, a sufficient cause of crime in Merton's formulation.

In light of common misinterpretations and misapplications of Merton's argument, it is important to underscore the point, as Merton does himself, that anomie theory is not a simple economic deprivation perspective on crime. Structural deprivation or inequality produces pressures to deviate under very specific cultural circumstances. Merton maintains that the relationship between deprivation and crime is high where there is great "cultural emphasis on mone-tary accumulation as a symbol of success," such as in the United States, and low where there is not.[39] In short, for Merton, culture conditions the impact of social structure on crime.[40] Less well developed in Merton's theory, yet equally impor-tant for explaining macrolevel variations in crime rates, is how social structure conditions or mediates the effect of culture on crime. We develop the latter point in detail in our discussion of the cultural and social sources of crime in the next chapter. However, before presenting our argument, which draws heavily on the anomie perspective, it is necessary to address some of the more important criticisms of anomie theory in general and of Merton's explanation of crime in the United States in particular.

Criticisms of Anomie Theory

Merton's formulation of the anomie perspective and his application of the perspective to the American crime problem have been heavily criticized. Some of the criticisms are, to be sure, friendly in nature and have served to expand and ultimately strengthen the theory by incorporating ideas from other perspectives. The most important of these are the contributions of Albert Cohen, and Richard Cloward and Lloyd Ohlin.[41] Both contributions emphasize the importance of subcultural adaptations by lower- and working-class youth to the problem of limited access to legitimate opportunities for success. Neither fundamentally challenges the premises of cultural universalism and structural inequality that underlie the anomie perspective. The criminologist Francis Cullen has suggested that Cohen's and Cloward and Ohlin's works (the latter, in particular) represent a significant break with "stress" theories of deviant or criminal motivations, such as Merton's, in their emphasis on explaining the alternative forms deviant adaptations may assume under varying structural and cultural conditions.[42] However, as we pointed out earlier, the general idea that cultural adaptations arise under specific structural circumstances and that structural pressures are culturally mediated is consistent with Merton's view of the two components of social organization as variable and interactive—and is missing from cultural or control perspectives.

Many other criticisms of Merton's argument have been far less friendly. Four of these criticisms stand out as both important in their own right and highly relevant to the purposes of the present volume:[43]

1. Merton assumes that value consensus exists in society and that the goal of monetary success is supreme. In fact, other goals are equally important, if not more important, for many Americans, and no single value pattern dominates American culture.

2. Merton's formulation of the crime problem is class biased. His explanation cannot explain the crimes of the rich and powerful. Moreover, the high frequency of such crimes constitutes empirical disconfirmation of the theory.

3. Merton fails to draw out the radical policy implications of his argument; he erroneously implies that liberal social reform (that is, providing greater equality of opportunity) offers a realistic solution to the crime problem in the United States.

4. Finally, Merton does not provide a precise definition of anomie. Alternatively, the conception of anomie that is discernible in his theory differs significantly from, and is inferior to, Durkheim's original formulation.

The first of these criticisms is based, in our view, on a caricature of Merton's position. Merton does not assume complete value consensus, nor does he assert that monetary success is the only meaningful goal in American culture. To the contrary, he explicitly disavows such a simpleminded position, stating that it would be "fanciful to assert that accumulated wealth stands alone as a symbol of success."[44] Rather, his point is that monetary success enjoys a position of special prominence in the hierarchy of goals in the United States and serves as a common benchmark for determining achievement. This assumption strikes us as a very reasonable one, and it has been backed up by research on the social meanings of success. This research reveals that material well-being is indeed the principal standard used in popular judgments of social standing in America.[45]

The criticism that anomie theory is class biased also reflects a somewhat oversimplified reading of Merton's arguments. It is true that Merton concentrates on the criminal behavior of the lower classes in explicating the implications of his theory for the social distribution of crime in American society. However, his basic argument can be extended to explain criminal behavior among those at the upper levels of the social hierarchy as well. A good illustration of this type of extension is provided in the work of Nikos Passas. Passas describes the strain toward anomie experienced by corporate executives, individuals who are under severe pressures to maximize profits under conditions of structural constraints. Such a situation, Passas suggests, is conducive to "organizational innovation"—high levels of corporate deviance and white-collar crime. Passas thus explains how both upper- and lower-class crimes can be accounted for by reference to the very same mechanisms, mechanisms that are described in the general anomie perspective.[46]

More important for present purposes, Merton's theory should not be reduced to his explanation of the social distribution of crime. Merton actually advances two related but distinct explanations of crime. One concerns the social distribution of crime within a society, but the other pertains to variation in levels of crime across societies. Although the former has received far greater attention than the latter from researchers and other theorists—and is the primary basis for the conversion of anomie theory into strain theory—the two explanations are in fact separable. This means that conceptual and empirical challenges to one are not necessarily damaging to the other. We draw most directly on those aspects of Merton's arguments that deal with variation in crime rates across rather than within societies, and hence the class-bias criticism is not directly relevant to our analysis.[47]

In contrast, we find merit in the third criticism of Merton's thesis, that he and his followers fail to recognize fully the radical policy implications of the anomie perspective on crime. Merton often is faulted for being politically naive when considering the prospects for implementing greater equality of opportunity in American society. As Vold and Bernard remind us, "Patterns of self-interest always develop around existing social structural arrangements," and those who benefit from the status quo are likely to resist efforts at social change and to have the political resources to do so effectively.[48]

In our view, however, a more fundamental criticism can be leveled at the liberal policy implications typically associated with Merton's theory: They do not really follow from the theory itself. If the American Dream places a heavy cultural emphasis on monetary success at any cost for everyone in society, then those who are unsuccessful in the pursuit of material well-being will be pressured to use illegitimate means regardless of the "openness" of the opportunity structure. The realization of a perfect meritocracy with full equality of opportunity would not eliminate the cultural pressures for crime. It would mainly redistribute the pressures to different individuals, those who lack the skills and talents that are rewarded in the marketplace.[49] Hence, expanding opportunities to disadvantaged segments of the population, however desirable in its own right, is not a crime reduction strategy that necessarily follows from Merton's theory.

The fourth criticism often leveled at Merton, that his use of the concept of anomie is not always clear, also has considerable merit. Anomie appears to have two distinct meanings in Merton's formulation. One is the rather standard reference to the weakening of the regulatory force of social norms, in other words, "normlessness." In this sense, anomie might be viewed as indicating the absence of culture. An alternative view, which has been formulated very effectively by Marco Orru, is that anomie is an important product of culture.[50] Specifically, anomie may be seen as a "value" to be inculcated along with others by the culture of modern capitalism—one that prescribes a high level of normative flexibility in the pursuit of dominant cultural goals. Merton hints at both of these meanings of anomie, and both are also contained in Durkheim's earlier discussion of the anomic consequences of modernization.

The modern capitalist economy, Durkheim observed, is in a chronic state of deregulation. Industrialization removed traditional social controls on aspirations; the limitless and inherently frustrating pursuit of material and social rewards is now defined as morally obligatory. In his classic study *Suicide,* Durkheim writes:

> It is everlastingly repeated that it is man's nature to be eternally
> dissatisfied, constantly to advance, without relief or rest, toward an
> indefinite goal. The longing for infinity is daily represented as a mark of
> moral distinction.[51]

Anomie refers to the social conditions that characterize this "longing for infinity." They include not only the breakdown of traditional social controls, or the failure to replace them with new ones, but also new standards and symbols of personal achievement. For Durkheim, anomie is both the weakening of traditional moral regulation and a new kind of morality. It is the morality of modern capitalism—an open and peculiarly permissive morality, without doubt, but one that nevertheless functions to motivate conduct. Limitless achievement is not simply what is exposed by the removal of traditional social constraints; it is itself an "ethic" that must be culturally motivated and socially sustained. In sum, for both Merton and Durkheim the deregulation of behavior does not result only from the passing of traditional society; it is part of the cultural context of capitalist society.

The fundamental question for Durkheim was whether modern societies could develop new forms of control to limit the very "appetites" that they helped to stimulate. He suggested specific institutional changes, such as the formation of occupational communities and the enhancement of the moral force of the state, to bring the new controls into being. This is where Merton makes his decisive break with Durkheim. Merton fails to extend his conception of social structure beyond the class system. The function of social structure, for Merton, is to distribute opportunities to achieve cultural goals. However, as Durkheim recognized, there is more to social structure than this. Social structure also functions to place limits on certain cultural imperatives so that they do not dominate and ultimately destroy others. This is the specific role of social institutions. However, Merton devotes little attention to institutions, beyond the system of social stratification, in his discussion of social structure and anomie.

The basic shortcoming remaining in Merton's explanation of crime, and in the anomie tradition more generally, is the absence of a comprehensive theory of institutional structure and functioning. The major purpose of the next chapter is to begin to fill this gap in the anomie tradition and, in so doing, to realize more fully the promise of the sociological paradigm for the study of crime.

NOTES

1. Short (1985, p. 51).
2. See Bailey (1987, pp. 24–26) for a discussion of the role of paradigms in social science.
3. See Short (1985) and Cohen (1985).
4. See Turk (1969) for a classic analysis of the general process of criminalization. Gove, Hughes, and Geerken (1985) and O'Brien (1985) offer insightful discussions of the measurement of crime.
5. Durkheim defines "social facts" in *The Rules of Sociological Method* ([1895] 1964b). He applies the idea of social facts to what is commonly viewed as a quintessential individual act—the taking of one's own life—in his classic work Suicide ([1897] 1966). Beeghley (2003, pp. 23-38) illustrates nicely the application of the Durkheimian perspective on "social facts" to the phenomenon of contemporary homicide rates.
6. The data in Figure 3.1 exclude persons who were on leave, retired, in school, or keeping house. The GSS data are from *MicroCase* version 4.8.
7. The correlation is Pearson's *r*, which varies from a value of zero to 1.00 or -1.00, with zero indicating no relationship, and 1.00 and -1.00 indicating a perfect positive or negative relationship, respectively. The relationship between the unemployment rate and the percentage of the population with a college degree shown in Figure 3.2 is not significantly different from zero, meaning that the chances are very good that there is no relationship between the two measures for a longer period than the period from which the sample was drawn.
   The trend data on unemployment and educational attainment were retrieved

online at http://www.census.gov/prod/2004pubs/03statab/labor.pdf; http://www.census.gov/prod/2002pubs/01statab/labor.pdf; http://www.census.gov/prod/2004pubs/03statab/edu.pdf. For a discussion of macrolevel unemployment trends, see Samuelson and Nordhaus (1989, chap. 13).

8. The data are from *MicroCase*.

9. Hodgins (1992, p. 482).

10. See Cohen (1985, pp. 230–231) for a general discussion of the interrelationships between individual- and macrolevel theorizing in criminology.

11. This conception of the seriousness of crimes is consistent with the approach taken by criminologists who have scaled different crime types according to their perceived seriousness based on ratings from general population surveys. See, for example, Rossi et al. (1974); Sellin and Wolfgang (1964); and Wolfgang et al. (1985).

12. The influence of methodological choices and constraints on data acquisition and theory formulation in criminology, and on the development of the highly influential "control" perspective in particular, is revealed in an interview with Travis Hirschi: "Control theory as I stated it cannot really be understood unless one takes into account the fact that I was attached to a particular method of research. When I was working on the theory, I knew that my data were going to be survey data; therefore I knew that I was going to have mainly the perceptions, attitudes, and values of individuals as reported by them. . . . Had I data on other people, or on the structure of the community, I would have had to state the theory in a quite different way" (quoted in Lilly, Cullen, and Ball, 1989, p. 105). Stitt and Giacopassi (1992, p. 4) speculate that the most likely reason for the dominance of social control theory in criminology for several decades is that "Hirschi's version was directly operationally defined in a survey format."

13. Rosenberg and Mercy (1986, p. 376). See also Hemenway (2004).

14. The data on cause of death are for 2001. The nonfatal injury data are for 2002. The data were obtained from the National Center for Injury Prevention and Control of the Centers for Disease Control (CDC) (http://www.cdc.gov/ncipc/wisqars).

15. Gottfredson and Hirschi (1990).

16. van Dijk and Kangaspunta (2000, p. 39).

17. Parsons (1951) characterizes culture as the "symbolic-meaningful" realm of social organization. The concept of a social institution is explained in Chapter 4.

18. See Bernard (1995), Cullen (1983), and Messner (1988).

19. Braithwaite (1989) includes labeling theory in his broad etiological framework for understanding crime and social control. We have excluded biophysiological perspectives from our discussion. See Fishbein (1990), Grisolia et al. (1997), Raine (2002), and Wilson and Herrnstein (1985) for overviews of arguments and research on the relationship between biophysiological factors and criminality. Walters (1992) provides a systematic review of studies of the "gene-crime" relationship.

20. Sutherland (1947, p. 7).

21. Sellin, quoted in Sykes and Cullen (1992, p. 320n). In addition to Sutherland's theory of differential association, influential contributions to the cultural-social learning perspective include the reformulation of differential association theory in the terms of operant conditioning theory by Burgess and Akers (1966; see also Akers et al., 1979); Curtis's (1975) discussion of violent subcultures among urban blacks, and

Anderson's (1999) work on the "code of the street"; the "Southern subculture of violence" hypothesis as developed by Gastil (1971) and Hackney (1969; see Hawley and Messner [1989] for a detailed overview of theory and research in this area); Miller's (1958) discussion of crime and lower-class culture; and Wolfgang and Ferracuti's (1967) classic statement of the "subculture of violence" thesis. Although not intended as an explanation of crime, but rather of the persistence of poverty, Oscar Lewis's (1966) idea of a "culture of poverty" figures importantly in criticisms of cultural deviance theory.

22. Kornhauser (1978, p. 196) has remarked, "In Sutherland's world rules are never willfully violated." Kornhauser's (1978) *Social Sources of Delinquency* and Hirschi's (1969) *Causes of Delinquency* remain the most important theoretical critiques of the cultural deviance perspective.

23. Kornhauser (1978, pp. 9–10).

24. van den Haag (1978, p. 210).

25. See Rosenfeld (1989, pp. 456–457).

26. See Hirschi (1969). This section draws heavily on Rosenfeld (1989, p. 457). The imagery of human nature underlying control theory—the "Hobbesian ontology"—is grounded in the classic contribution of Thomas Hobbes ([1651] 1958).

27. For a description of the Chicago School's analysis of urban social and ecological dynamics, see Park, Burgess, and McKenzie ([1925] 1967). See Shaw and McKay (1969) for a description of the sources and consequences of social disorganization in neighborhoods. Bursik and Grasmick (1993) refer to neighborhood criminology and neighborhood theories of crime in their study of community crime control. Sampson, Morenoff, and Gannon-Rowley (2002) provide a comprehensive review of the contemporary research on "neighorhood effects" on crime.

28. Good discussions of changes and continuities in disorganization theory include Bursik (1988), Bursik and Grasmick (1993), Sampson and Groves (1989), Sampson, Raudenbush, and Earls (1997), and Stark (1987). One of the more important elaborations of the classical social disorganization perspective is "routine activities" theory. The central claim of this perspective is that opportunities for successful criminal victimization vary along with normal patterns of social interaction (for example, work and leisure). Crime occurs when motivated offenders come into contact with suitable targets (persons or property) in situations where "guardians" are unable to intervene to protect the targets of crime. See Cohen and Felson (1979); Felson (1998).

29. The classic account is that of Mills (1943).

30. Kornhauser (1978, p. 13).

31. Kornhauser (1978, p. 13).

32. See Kroeber and Parsons (1958).

33. From the 1939 edition of Sutherland's textbook, quoted in Vold and Bernard (1986, p. 212).

34. See Vold and Bernard (1986, pp. 212–213).

35. See Kornhauser (1978, pp. 62–82).

36. Notable efforts to bring together different theories of crime within a single explanatory framework include the explanation of delinquency and drug use developed by Delbert Elliott and colleagues (Elliott, Huizinga, and Ageton, 1985); Hagan, Simpson, and

Gillis's (1987) "power-control" explanation of gender and crime (see also Colvin and Pauly, 1983); John Braithwaite's (1989) theory of crime and "reintegrative shaming"; and Charles Tittle's (1995) "control balance theory." For a critique of attempts at theoretical synthesis or integration in criminology, see Hirschi (1979, 1989).

37. Kornhauser (1978, p. 69).
38. See Merton (1938, 1959, 1964; 1968, pp. 185–248).
39. Merton (1938, pp. 680–681).
40. See Messner (1988, pp. 47–49) for an elaboration of this point.
41. Cohen (1955); Cloward and Ohlin (1960).
42. Cullen (1983, 1988).
43. Excellent discussions of these and related criticisms of Merton's theory may be found in Clinard (1964), Bernard (1984), Pfohl (1985, pp. 210–239), and Vold, Bernard, and Snipes (2002, pp. 145-147).
44. Merton (1968, p. 190).
45. See Rainwater (1974) and Coleman and Rainwater (1978).
46. Passas (1990; 1997). See also Cohen (1995) and Vaughn (1983).
47. See Messner (1988).
48. Vold and Bernard (1986, pp. 202–203).
49. See especially Vold and Bernard (1986, p. 203).
50. Orru (1987, pp. 142–143).
51. Durkheim ([1897] 1966, p. 257).

4

Culture, Institutional Structure, and Crime

America has always been the most competitive of societies. It poises
its citizens against one another, with the warning that they must make
it on their own. Hence the stress on moving past others, driven by a
fear of falling behind. No other nation so rates its residents as winners
or losers.

ANDREW HACKER, TWO NATIONS: BLACK AND WHITE, SEPARATE, HOSTILE,
UNEQUAL [1]

The best minds are not in government. If any were, business would hire
them away.

RONALD REAGAN,
(40TH PRESIDENT OF THE UNITED STATES) [2]

In August 1974, under threat of impeachment, Richard Nixon resigned from
the office of President of the United States. Tom Wicker, in his book *One of
Us: Richard Nixon and the American Dream,* speculates about the reasons for
Nixon's continuing popularity, even after most Americans had been convinced
of his crimes. Wicker suggests that Nixon may have represented a national self-
assessment. Americans may have seen reflected in him

> their own melancholy knowledge, hard earned in a demanding world,
> that ideals had to yield to necessity, right to might, compassion
> to interest, principle to circumstance. They might even have understood
> that Nixon, or anyone, could believe himself forced on occasion to cheat
> a little, lie a little, find an edge, get out front of more favored

competitors any way he could—as they themselves had done, or would do—in the unrelenting battles of life. . . . If, as president, he swore to uphold the Constitution but skirted it when he could, that was American still; which of us in the national rush to get ahead has never cut a corner or winked at the law?[3]

In Wicker's view, Nixon was not an American aberration but a reflection of fundamental features of American society.

Although his misdeeds were not motivated by economic concerns in the narrow sense, Nixon's actions and his character, Wicker suggests, are best understood in terms of the logic and language of the marketplace. In the "rush to get ahead," it is sometimes necessary to "find an edge," "cut a corner," bend "principle to circumstance," "cheat a little," "lie a little." These are actions and motivations that ordinary Americans can understand, if not condone, because they too inhabit the tough, competitive social terrain described by Tom Wicker and Andrew Hacker (quoted above)—a world of "unrelenting battles" in which the "fear of falling behind" drives combatants to adopt the survival ethic of "do unto others before they do unto you." Nixon's story, in short, is a paradigm of the social forces conducive to crime in the United States.

In this chapter, we explicate and illustrate these criminogenic forces, and in so doing we advance a sociological explanation for the high rates of crime in American society. We hypothesize that the American Dream itself exerts pressures toward crime by encouraging an anomic cultural environment, an environment in which people are encouraged to adopt an "anything goes" mentality in the pursuit of personal goals. Furthermore, we argue that the anomic pressures inherent in the American Dream are nourished and sustained by a distinctive *institutional balance of power* dominated by the economy. The interplay between the core cultural commitments of the American Dream and its companion institutional balance of power results in widespread anomie, weak social controls, diminished social support, and, ultimately, high levels of crime.

To develop these arguments, we begin this chapter with a detailed discussion of the value orientations underlying the American Dream and the ways in which this value complex is conducive to an anomic environment. We then discuss the nature of social institutions, the interdependencies among institutions, and the interrelationships between culture and institutional structure. Finally, we explore the consequences of the cultural and institutional organization of American society for patterns of and trends in serious crime.

THE VALUE FOUNDATIONS OF THE AMERICAN DREAM

Robert Heilbroner has asked

> Who has not reflected on the question of why the Japanese are so different from ourselves? Or the Swedes or the Italians, the French or the Germans? The answer that we give to this question is that their "cultures" are different, which indeed they are, but different in what ways?[4]

Robert Merton, in his essay "Social Structure and Anomie," provides a useful starting point for formulating an answer to Heilbroner's question about the distinctiveness of American culture. According to Merton, the cultural ethos of the American Dream sets the United States apart from other modern industrial nations. Merton himself does not provide a formal definition of the American Dream, but it is possible to formulate a reasonably concise characterization of this cultural orientation based on Merton's discussion of American culture in general, his scattered references to the American Dream, and the commentary of others on Merton's work.[5] Our definition, which we introduced in Chapter 1, is as follows: The American Dream refers to a commitment to the goal of material success, to be pursued by everyone in society, under conditions of open, individual competition.

The American Dream is a powerful force in our society because it embodies the basic value commitments of the culture: its achievement orientation, individualism, universalism, and peculiar form of materialism that has been described as the "fetishism of money."[6] Each of these value orientations contributes to the anomic character of the American Dream: its strong emphasis on the importance of realizing cultural goals in comparison with its relatively weak emphasis on the importance of using the legitimate means to do so.

Before examining the value complex underlying the American Dream, we caution against an overly simplistic interpretation of American culture. The United States is a complex and, in many respects, culturally pluralistic society. It neither contains a single, monolithic value system nor exhibits complete consensus surrounding specific value orientations. Historically, certain groups have been completely excluded from the American Dream. An obvious example is that of enslaved African-Americans in the antebellum South. In addition, cultural prescriptions and mandates are filtered through prevailing gender roles. Indeed, we argue later in this chapter that the interpretation of the American Dream differs to some extent for men and women. We nevertheless concur with Jennifer Hochschild's claim that the American Dream has been, and continues to be, a "defining characteristic of American culture," a cultural ethos "against which all competitors must contend."[7] An adequate understanding of the crime problem in the United States, therefore, is impossible without reference to the cluster of values underlying the American Dream: achievement, individualism, universalism, and materialism.

Achievement

A defining feature of American culture is its strong achievement orientation. People are encouraged to make something of themselves, to set goals, and to strive to reach them. At the same time, personal worth tends to be evaluated on the basis of the outcome of these efforts. Success, in other words, is to a large extent the ultimate measure of a person's value. As Marco Orru explains

> The measure of individuals' social esteem is not provided by their position in the social system according to inherited status, to their location in social networks or to other ascribed traits; instead, one's own talents as measured by individual achievement are the predominant (if not the only) standard of judgment.[8]

Given such a value orientation, the failure to achieve readily equates with a failure to make any meaningful contribution to society at all. The cultural pressures to achieve at any cost are thus very intense. In this way, a strong achievement orientation, at the level of basic cultural values, is highly conducive to the mentality that "it's not how you play the game; it's whether you win or lose."[9]

Individualism

A second basic value orientation at the core of American culture is individualism. Americans are deeply committed to individual rights and individual autonomy. Bellah and his colleagues, in their book *Habits of the Heart,* describe the centrality of individualism to the American identity in these terms:

> [Americans] believe in the dignity, indeed the sacredness, of the individual. Anything that would violate our right to think for ourselves, judge for ourselves, make our own decisions, live our lives as we see fit, is not only morally wrong, it is sacrilegious.[10]

This obsession with the individual, when combined with the strong achievement orientation in American culture, exacerbates the tendency toward anomie. In the pursuit of success, people are encouraged to "make it" on their own. Fellow members of society thus become competitors and rivals in the struggle to achieve social rewards and, ultimately, to validate personal worth. The intense individual competition to succeed pressures people to disregard normative restraints on behavior when these restraints threaten to interfere with the realization of personal goals.[11]

Universalism

A third basic value orientation in American culture is universalism. Socialization into the cultural goals of American society has a decidedly democratic quality. With few exceptions, everyone is encouraged to aspire to social ascent, and everyone is susceptible to evaluation on the basis of individual achievements.

An important corollary of this universal entitlement to dream about success is that the hazards of failure are also universal. Because virtually no one is exempt from the cultural mandate for individual achievement, the anomic pressures associated with an individualistic achievement orientation permeate, albeit with varying degrees of intensity, the entire social structure.

The "Fetishism" of Money

Finally, in American culture, success is signified in a distinctive way: by the accumulation of monetary rewards. Money is awarded special priority in American culture. As Merton observes, "In some large measure, money has been consecrated as a value in itself, over and above its expenditure for articles of consumption or its use for the enhancement of power." The point to emphasize here is not that Americans are uniquely materialistic, for a strong interest in material well-being can be found in most societies. Rather, the distinctive feature of American culture is the preeminent role of money as the "metric" of success. Orru succinctly expresses the idea in the following terms: "Money is literally, in this context, a *currency* for measuring achievement."[12]

There is an important implication of the signification of achievement with reference to monetary rewards. Monetary success is inherently open-ended. It is always possible in principle to have more money. Hence, the American Dream offers "no final stopping point." It requires "never-ending achievement."[13] The pressure to accumulate money is therefore relentless, which entices people to pursue their monetary goals by any means necessary. A 17-year-old African-American interprets Malcolm X's use of the expression "by any means necessary" in just these materialistic terms:

> Malcolm is saying that it's about power. We can go to school and study and try to get power. Or we can take it and get violent if you push us to the edge. If we get jobs and money, we'll march your march and talk your talk. It's not a black-white thing, it's a green thing.

The media play a pivotal role in cultivating these anomic pressures associated with a consumerist culture. As one social critic observes,

> Perhaps television's influence stems not from specific programming content, but from its being a major component in the American, and indeed now the international, way of life. The commercial medium is designed to sell, everything from the audiences sought by advertisers to the expensive sneakers sought by youngsters, many of whom will do whatever is necessary to get them. They have been insistently persuaded that their lives are nothing without these athlete-sponsored products.[14]

In sum, the dominant value patterns of American culture—specifically, its achievement orientation, its competitive individualism, its universalism in goal orientations and evaluative standards, when harnessed to the preeminent goal of monetary success—crystallize into the distinctive cultural ethos of the American Dream. The American Dream, in turn, encourages members of society to pursue ends, in Merton's words, "limited only by considerations of technical expediency."[15] This open, widespread, competitive, and anomic quest for success provides a cultural environment highly conducive to criminal behavior.

Cultural forces thus play a prominent role in our explanation of the high levels of crime in American society. However, a complete sociological explanation of crime must extend beyond features of culture and incorporate social structural factors as well. Culture does not exist in isolation from social structure but rather is expressed in, reproduced by, and occasionally impeded by social structure. Any comprehensive explanation that emphasizes "culture" as a cause of crime must therefore also consider the relevant range of structural conditions through which the cultural sources of crime are enacted. In our view, the most important of these structural conditions are the institutional arrangements of society.

THE INSTITUTIONAL STRUCTURE OF AMERICAN SOCIETY

In Chapter 2, we discussed the relationship between crime and what we referred to as "local institutions" without offering a definition of social institutions or an account of their functions at the level of entire social systems. Although this informal usage was appropriate for our descriptive purposes in that discussion, we must now discuss social institutions more fully and specify systematically the impact on crime of the institutional structure of society.

The Nature and Functioning of Social Institutions

Social institutions are the building blocks of whole societies. As such, they constitute the basic subject matter of macrolevel analysis. Sociology textbooks commonly define institutions as "relatively stable sets of norms and values, statuses and roles, and groups and organizations" that regulate human conduct to meet the basic needs of a society.[16] Institutions are "accretive" social formations; they tend to develop slowly and continuously, seemingly without conscious purpose or design. They allow a society to endure over time despite the constant coming and going of individual members. In the words of the influential sociological theorist Talcott Parsons, "Institutional patterns are the 'backbone' of the social system."[17]

The functions of institutions in social systems have been compared with the functions of *instincts* in biological organisms: Both channel behavior to meet basic system needs. However, as the sociologist Peter Berger has pointed out, this comparison reveals not only the functional equivalence but also a basic structural difference between institutions and instincts. Human beings need institutions precisely because we cannot rely on "instinct" for complex social behavior. Compared with other species, humans are instinctually underdeveloped.

Therefore, we must depend on institutions for our individual and collective survival. This institutional dependence has profound implications for the motivation and control of human social behavior, including criminal behavior.[18]

The basic social needs around which institutions develop include the need to (1) adapt to the environment, (2) mobilize and deploy resources for the achievement of collective goals, and (3) socialize members to accept the society's fundamental normative patterns.[19]

Adaptation to the environment is the primary responsibility of economic institutions. The *economy* consists of activities organized around the production and distribution of goods and services. It functions to satisfy the basic material requirements for human existence, such as the need for food, clothing, and shelter.

The political system, or *polity,* mobilizes and distributes power to attain collective goals. One collective purpose of special importance is the maintenance of public safety. Political institutions are responsible for "protecting members of society from invasions from without, controlling crime and disorder within, and providing channels for resolving conflicts of interest."[20] As part of the polity, agencies of the civil and criminal justice systems have major responsibility for crime control and the lawful resolution of conflicts.

The institution of the *family* bears primary responsibility for the regulation of sexual activity and for the replacement of members of society. These tasks involve establishing and enforcing the limits of legitimate sexual relations among adults, the physical care and nurturing of children, and the socialization of children into the values, goals, and beliefs of the dominant culture. Families also bear much of the responsibility for the care of dependent persons in society more generally (for example, caring for the infirm and the elderly). In addition, a particularly important function of the family in modern societies is to provide emotional support for its members. To a significant degree, the family serves as a refuge from the tensions and stresses generated in other institutional domains. In this idea of the family as a "haven" from the rigors of the public world lies the implicit recognition of the need to counterbalance and temper the harsh, competitive conditions of public life.[21] These protective functions of the family traditionally have had greater salience for men. In addition, the family generates its own pressures and conflicts, and these have a special impact on women, the traditional caretakers of domestic life.

The institution of *education* shares many of the socialization functions of the family. Like the family, schools are given responsibility for transmitting basic cultural standards to new generations. In modern industrial societies, schools are also oriented toward the specific task of preparing youth for the demands of adult roles, in particular, occupational roles. In addition, education aims to enhance personal adjustment, facilitate the development of individual human potential, and advance the general knowledge base of the culture.

These four social institutions—the economy, the polity, the family, and education—comprise the central focus of our analysis of crime. They do not, of course, exhaust the institutional structure of modern societies, nor are they the only institutions with relevance to crime. Religion and mass communications, for example, have been the subjects of important criminological research.[22] However, the economy, the polity, the family, and education are, in our view, central to what may be called an "institutional understanding" of crime.

Social institutions are to some extent distinct with respect to the primary activities around which they are organized. At the same time, however, the functions of institutions overlap and depend on one another. The functioning of each institution has consequences for the functioning of the others. For example, the performance of the economy depends on the quality of the "human capital" cultivated in the schools. The capacity of the schools to develop human capital is circumscribed by the individual backgrounds that students bring with them from their families, what Pierre Bourdieu refers to as "cultural capital."[23] The effective functioning of all three of these institutions—the economy, education, and the family—presupposes an environment with at least a modicum of social order, for which the polity has formal responsibility. Finally, the effectiveness of the polity in promoting the collective good depends on the nature and quality of economic resources and human capabilities supplied by the other institutions.

The interdependence of major social institutions implies that, for the society to "work" at all, some coordination and cooperation must exist among institutions. The requirements for the effective functioning of any given institution, however, may conflict with the requirements of another. This potential for conflict is illustrated by the particularly stark contrast between the dominant values embodied in the institutions of the economy and the family. Family relationships are expected to be regulated by the norm of *particularism,* whereas transactions in the marketplace are supposed to be governed by *universalism.* Earl Babbie provides an amusing illustration of the distinction between these two value orientations:

> If you go into a supermarket to buy a loaf of bread, the various checkers are fundamentally interchangeable. You can purchase the bread equally well from any of the checkers, so you choose the check-out line that is the most convenient for you (for example, nearest, shortest).
>
> By contrast, suppose you are a parent with a young child in preschool. When you arrive at the classroom after the end of the school day, it would not be considered appropriate for you to simply pick up the most convenient child. Instead, you are expected to take a *particular* child home: *your own.*[24]

As this example suggests, economic life and family life are supposed to be governed by fundamentally different standards in modern industrial societies. Positions and roles in the family are allocated, in large measure, on the basis of ascribed characteristics. Each member is entitled to special considerations by virtue of his or her unique identity and place in the family unit. In contrast, economic relationships, such as transactions in the marketplace, are supposed to entail universalistic orientations, and economic positions are supposed to be filled according to achievement criteria. Persons who occupy the same or functionally equivalent statuses are to be treated similarly, and access to these statuses is supposed to be gained by demonstrating the capacity to perform successfully the associated duties and responsibilities. Thus, an inevitable tension arises between the kinds of value orientations required for the effective functioning of the family and those required for the efficient functioning of a market economy.[25]

Any given society therefore will be characterized by a distinctive arrangement of social institutions that reflects a balancing of the sometimes competing claims and requisites of the different institutions, yielding a distinctive institutional balance of power. Further, the nature of the resulting configuration of institutions intimately relates to the larger culture. Indeed, our basic premise about social organization posits that culture and the institutional balance of power are mutually reinforcing. On the one hand, culture influences the character of institutions and their positions relative to one another. Culture is, in a sense, "given life" in the institutional structure of society. On the other hand, the patterns of social relationships constituting institutions reproduce and sustain cultural commitments. This is, ultimately, where culture "comes from."

We are well aware of the ideal typical nature of this description of institutional functioning. For example, occupational roles are often filled on the basis of functionally irrelevant criteria (such as race and gender), even in societies that proclaim open competition and equal opportunity for all members. Moreover, the persistence of ascriptive inequalities in societies formally committed to the norm of equal opportunity may give rise to feelings of injustice and dissatisfaction that promote criminal behavior. Our present concern, however, is not with how *departures* from cultural ideals influence crime rates but with how crime is produced when societies work pretty much the way they are supposed to.[26] In the section that follows, we discuss the type of institutional structure that is supportive of and compatible with the distinctive elements of American culture, an institutional structure characterized by the dominance of the economy.

The American Dream and the Institutional Balance of Power

The core elements of the American Dream—a strong achievement orientation, a commitment to competitive individualism, universalism, and, most important, the glorification of material success—have their institutional underpinnings in the economy. The salient feature of the economy of the United States is its capitalist nature. Private ownership and control of property, and free-market mechanisms for the production and distribution of goods and services, are the defining characteristics of a capitalist society.

These structural arrangements encourage and presuppose certain cultural orientations. For the economy to operate efficiently, the private owners of property must be profit oriented and eager to invest, and workers must be willing to exchange their labor for wages. The motivational mechanism of the promise of financial returns underlies these conditions. The internal logic of a capitalist economy thus presumes that an attraction to monetary rewards as a result of achievement in the marketplace is widely diffused throughout the population.[27]

A capitalist economy is also highly competitive for all those involved, property owners and workers alike. Firms unable to adapt to shifting consumer demands or to fluctuations in the business cycle will likely face failure. Workers who cannot keep up with changing skill requirements or who are unproductive in comparison with others are likely to be fired. This intense competition discourages economic actors from becoming wedded to conventional ways of doing things and instead encourages them to substitute new techniques for traditional ones if these techniques offer advantages in meeting economic goals. Therefore, a capitalist economy naturally cultivates a competitive, innovative spirit.

The distinctive feature of the United States, however, is the *exaggerated* emphasis on monetary success and the *unrestrained* receptivity to innovation. The goal of monetary success overwhelms other goals and becomes the principal measuring rod for achievements. The resulting proclivity and pressures to innovate resist any regulation not justified by purely technical considerations. The obvious question arises: Why have cultural orientations that express the inherent logic of capitalism evolved to a particularly extreme degree in American society? The answer, we submit, lies in the inability of other social institutions to tame economic imperatives. In short, the institutional balance of power is tilted toward the economy.

The historical evidence suggests that this distinctive institutional structure has always existed in the United States. In his analysis of American slavery, the historian Stanley Elkins observes that capitalism emerged "as the principal dynamic force in American society," free to develop according to its own institutional logic without interference from "prior traditional institutions, with competing claims of their own." Whereas capitalism developed in European societies (and later in Japan) within powerful preexisting institutional frameworks, the institutional structure of American society emerged simultaneously with, and was profoundly shaped by, the requirements of capitalist economic development. American capitalism thus took on a "purity of form" unknown in other capitalist societies.[28] Moreover, other institutions were cast in distinctly subsidiary positions in relation to the economy.

In Elkins's view, by the 1830s many Americans could imagine that they had no need for "institutions" as such, which were regarded with suspicion as vestiges of an older, oppressive social order. Capitalism represented not a new type of social organization, in this view, but a liberation of the individual from social organization itself. The sources of social stability were to be found not in society but in human nature. The early American could believe that he did not

> draw from society his traditions, his culture, and all his aspirations; indeed he, the transcendent individual—the new symbol of virtue— now "confronted" society; he challenged it as something of a conspiracy to rob him of his birthright. Miraculously, all society then sprang to his aid in the celebration of that conceit.[29]

We must point out that Elkins's thesis does not support the simplistic assertion that "capitalism causes crime." Elkins himself calls attention to the fallacy in attributing the cultural and social characteristics of capitalist societies simply to the nature of capitalism:

> This idea cannot tell us much about the differences between two societies, both capitalist, but in one of which the "means of production" have changed into capitalistic ones and in the other of which the means of production were never anything but capitalistic and in which no other forces were present to resist their development.[30]

Similarly, Robert Heilbroner writes that "*American* capitalism, not American *capitalism*" is responsible for the features of our society that distinguish it, for better or worse, from other capitalist societies.[31] As we documented in Chapter 2, the combination of high levels of serious crime and mass incarceration represents a uniquely American phenomenon among modern capitalist societies. These features of our society, therefore, cannot be accounted for by capitalism alone. Variation in levels of crime and the societal response to crime are rooted, following Elkins, in their contrasting institutional settings.

Elkins's portrait of the barren institutional landscape of early American society may be somewhat overdrawn, and aspects of his analysis of the North American slave system are controversial.[32] In addition, his account of the early American and "his" traditions, "his" culture, and "his" liberation from social organization refers quite literally to the free, white, male population of the United States at the time. Nonetheless, we accept the basic argument that capitalism developed in the United States without the institutional restraints found in other societies. As a consequence, the economy assumed an unusual dominance in the institutional structure of society from the very beginning of the nation's history, and this distinctive institutional arrangement has continued to the present.

Our notion of economic dominance in the institutional balance of power resembles Elliott Currie's concept of a "market society" as distinct from a "market economy." According to Currie, in a market society "the pursuit of private gain becomes the organizing principle of all areas of social life—not simply a mechanism that we may use to accomplish certain circumscribed ends."[33] Economic dominance characteristic of the American market society manifests itself, we argue, in three interrelated ways:

1. devaluation of noneconomic institutional functions and roles,
2. accommodation to economic requirements by other institutions, and
3. penetration of economic norms into other institutional domains.

Devaluation   American society *devalues* noneconomic goals, positions, and roles relative to the ends and means of economic activity. The relative devaluation of the distinctive functions of education and of the social roles that fulfill these functions provides one example. Education is regarded largely as a means to occupational attainment, which in turn is valued primarily insofar as it promises economic rewards. Neither the acquisition of knowledge nor learning for its own sake is highly valued. An interview with a high school student whose grades dropped when she increased her schedule at her two after-school jobs to thirty hours a week provides a revealing illustration of the devaluation of education relative to purely monetary concerns. She described her feelings about the intrinsic rewards of education this way: "School's important but so's money. Homework doesn't pay. Teachers say education is your payment, and that just makes me want to puke."[34]

Given the relative devaluation of education, it is not surprising that effective performance of the roles involved with this activity does not confer particularly high status. The "good student" is not looked up to by his or her peers; the "master teacher" receives meager financial rewards and minimal public acclaim in comparison with those to be gained by success in business.

Similar processes are observed in the context of the family, although the tendency toward devaluation is perhaps not as pronounced as in other institutional arenas. There is a paradox here, because "family values" are typically extolled in public rhetoric. Nevertheless, family life has a tenuous position in American culture. It is the home*owner* rather than the home*maker* who is widely admired and envied—and whose image is reflected in the American Dream.

The lack of appreciation for the principal tasks of families—such as parenting, nurturing, and providing emotional support to others—is manifested in part in the low levels of compensation received by those who perform these tasks in the labor market. Consider the salaries for child-care providers. According to the 2000 National Compensation Survey of the U. S. Bureau of Labor Statistics, child-care workers ranked 401 out of 427 occupations with respect to hourly earnings. The mean hourly earnings for child-care workers amounted to $9.08 per hour. By contrast, the mean hourly earnings of animal caretakers, excluding farm animals, were $11.56. Those working within the child-care field have expressed considerable frustration over their unsuccessful efforts to secure higher wages. In the words of one nanny interviewed by *Newsweek*, "People don't want to pay what it takes to hire someone qualified." Kelly Campbell, president of the International Nanny Association, was even more blunt in her criticism of the unwillingness of most Americans to provide child-care workers with decent wages. Campbell warned that "until we get to the point where we value our children as much as our material possessions, we're going to have problems with child care."[35]

The relative devaluation of the family in comparison with the economy is not an inevitable consequence of the emergence of a modern industrial society, whether capitalist or socialist. The comparative criminologist Freda Adler points to nations such as Bulgaria, the (then) German Democratic Republic, Japan, Saudi Arabia, and Switzerland to illustrate the possibilities for maintaining a strong commitment to the family despite the profound social changes that accompany the transformation from agriculturally based economies to industrial economies. Each of these countries has made extensive and sometimes costly efforts to preserve the vitality of the family. Furthermore, these are precisely the kinds of societies that exhibit low crime rates and are not, in Adler's words, "obsessed with crime."[36]

The distinctive function of the polity, providing for the collective good, also tends to be devalued in comparison with economic functions, as suggested in the quotation at the beginning of this chapter from Ronald Reagan, a very popular two-term president in the 1980s. The general public has little regard for politics as an intrinsically valuable activity and confers little social honor on the role of the politician. Indeed, the label "politician" is commonly used in a disparaging way. Perhaps as a result, average citizens are not expected to be actively engaged in public service, which is left to those with a "career" in politics. The contrast with economic activity is illuminating. The citizen who refuses to vote may experience mild social disapproval; the able-bodied adult who refuses to work is socially degraded. Economic participation is obligatory for most adults. In contrast, even the minimal form of political participation entailed in voting (which has more in common with shopping than with work) is considered discretionary, and useful primarily to the extent that it leads to tangible economic rewards (for instance, lower taxes). Not surprisingly, compared with voters in other nations, a much smaller fraction of Americans turns out to vote. Only 58.3 percent of citizens in the voting-age population voted in the 2004 presidential election, about the same proportion as in the 2000 (59.5 percent) and 1996 (58.4 percent) presidential elections. Low rates of electoral participation in the United States are nothing new. In a comparison of voter turnout for national elections held during the 1970s in 90 nations, the United States ranked 73rd.[37]

The very purpose of government tends to be conceptualized in terms of its capacity to facilitate the individual pursuit of economic prosperity. The advice given to the Democratic ticket years ago in a presidential campaign by the conservative columnist George Will provides a good illustration. Will chastised liberal Democrats for their alleged preoccupation with issues of rights based on ethnicity and sexuality and advised the Democratic candidates to remember the following point that two popular former presidents, Franklin Roosevelt and Ronald Reagan, understood very well: "Americans are happiest when pursuing happiness, happiness understood as material advancement, pursued with government's help but not as a government entitlement."[38]

Will's advice to liberal Democrats reveals not only the core content of the American Dream and its effect on popular views of government, but a particular kind of collective "right" to which Americans are entitled: the right to consume.[39] Both of the major political parties celebrate the right to acquire material possessions; they differ mainly with respect to the proper degree of governmental involvement in expanding access to the means of consumption. No matter which party is in power, the function of government, at least in the domestic sphere, remains subsidiary to individual economic considerations.

Interestingly, one distinctive function of the polity does not appear to be generally devalued, namely, crime control. The American public predominantly agrees that government should undertake vigorous efforts to deal with the crime problem. If anything, Americans want government to do more to control crime. When respondents in the General Social Survey were asked about the appropriateness of government spending on "halting the rising crime rate," 56 percent responded that the government spends too little; only 7 percent stated that the government spends too much.[40] This eagerness to devote more tax dollars for purposes of "halting the rising crime rate" is particularly noteworthy, given that serious crime rates had actually been declining rather than rising at the time of the survey. Yet the selective valuation of the crime control function of government is compatible with the claim of economic dominance. Americans' obsession with crime is rooted in fears that crime threatens, according to political analyst Thomas Edsall, "their security, their values, their rights, and their livelihoods and the competitive prospects of their children." President Clinton used similar language when urging Congress to pass anticrime legislation during his first administration. In his weekly radio address, Clinton warned that, unless the rise in crime is halted, "we can't exercise the opportunities that there are for us, and our children can't inherit the American dream."[41] In other words, because crime control bears directly on the pursuit of the American Dream, this particular function of the polity receives high priority.

Accommodation   A second way in which the dominance of the economy manifests itself is in the *accommodations* that emerge in those situations where institutional claims are in competition. Economic conditions and requirements typically exert a much stronger influence on the operation of other institutions than vice versa. For example, the schedules, rewards, and penalties of the labor market dominate family routines. Roughly two-fifths of American workers now work a nonstandard schedule outside of the traditional 9-5 workday. As one consequence of such work schedules, a growing proportion of parents are not home together during the evening with their children, giving rise to a concern about declining "home-time" among U.S. families.[42] Whereas parents worry about finding time for their families, few workers must "find time" for their jobs. On the contrary, many feel fortunate that the economy has found time for them.

Consider the resistance to parental leave in the United States. Most industrialized nations mandate paid maternity or parental leave by law to enable parents to care for infants at home without threat of job loss. The data in Figure 4.1 indicate the stipulated duration of paid parental or maternity leave in the United States and the 16 advanced industrial nations whose crime rates were described in Chapter 2.[43] Of these nations, only the United States and Australia fail to provide for any mandatory paid leave. Legislation on family and emergency leave was signed into law in the United States in 1993 after a long political struggle, but this legislation only sets minimum standards for *unpaid,* not paid, leave, and only for workers in companies with 50 or more employees.

Most European nations implement additional policies that reflect a strong commitment to the institution of the family. These include direct cash allowances to families to cover some of the costs of child rearing, public childcare for young children, and universal access to health care to deal with the special needs of the very young and the elderly. In Italy, such policies are considered part of a mother's "birthright."[44] The contrast between the United States and another capitalist society with very low crime rates, Japan, is particularly striking in this regard. In Japan, business enterprises are accommodated to the needs of the

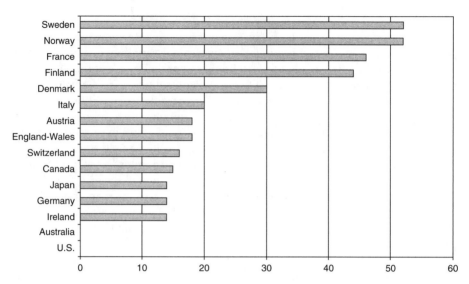

F I G U R E **4.1** Paid Parental Leave in 15 Advanced Nations, 1997–1999 (Number of Weeks)

family, becoming in some respects "surrogate families," with services ranging from child rearing to burial.[45]

The most important way that family life is influenced by the economy, however, is through the necessity for paid employment to support a family. Joblessness makes it difficult for families to remain intact or even to form in the first place. In the urban underclass, where rates of joblessness are chronically high, so too are rates of separation, divorce, single-parent households, and births to unmarried women.[46]

Educational institutions are also more likely to accommodate to the demands of the economy than is the economy to respond to the requirements of education. The timing of schooling reflects occupational demands rather than intrinsic features of the learning process or personal interest in the pursuit of knowledge. People go to school largely to prepare for "good" jobs. And once in the labor market, they have little opportunity to pursue further education for its own sake.

When workers do return to school, it is almost always to upgrade skills or credentials to keep pace with job demands, to seek higher-paying jobs, or to "retool" during spells of unemployment. A college admissions director observes that returning students are "hungry for practical education that they can take back to their workplace the next day." His university accommodates this demand by scheduling classes on Saturday, during the evening, and in shortened eight-week terms to ensure that education interferes as little as possible with students' work lives.[47]

At the organizational level, schools depend on the economy for financial resources. Private business is increasingly looked on as a savior of financially strapped public school systems. To illustrate, a school in New Jersey was able to maintain its gym by soliciting donations from a local business. A big sign subsequently adorned the school: "The Shoprite of Brookline Center." To be able to offer opportunities for field trips in an environment of meager state funding and citizens' resistance to higher local property taxes, some public schools have turned to a private Chicago company, the Field Trip Factory. The company arranges field trips to local stores and . . . "prepackages everything, from tour guide scripts to parental permission slips. Teachers love the convenience. Stingy school districts love the prices, especially when stores kick in the cost of the bus ride."[48]

To the extent that the viability of schools relies on the private sector, it is critical for school officials to convince business leaders that education is suitably responsive to business needs. It helps when some of the educators themselves are strongly oriented to monetary incentives. The president of Queens College of the City University of New York, an African-American physicist who financed his own education with scholarships, seemed undaunted by cuts in state funding for the school. Announcing a new campaign to increase alumni and corporate giving, he told a reporter: "One thing I learned growing up in the Bronx is that the only thing that matters is money. If you have a choice between love and money, take money—it's much more reliable."[49]

Of course, financial support to educational institutions from private business typically comes with strings attached, as illustrated in a controversial agreement that the University of California at Berkeley signed with the Swiss pharmaceutical firm Novartis in 1998. Novartis provided Berkeley with $25 million to fund basic research in the Department of Plant and Microbial Biology. In return, the private company was granted first rights to negotiate licenses for about a third of the discoveries in the department. More disturbing to some, however, was the decision to award two of the five seats on the department's research committee to representatives of Novartis. This committee oversees the spending of funds, and in so doing, helps set the research agenda. A professor of microbial ecology expressed concern about this type of "accommodation" to private industry:

> I'm not opposed to individual professors' serving as consultants
> to industry . . . If something goes wrong, it's their reputation that's
> at stake. But this is different. This deal institutionalizes the university's
> relationship with one company, whose interest is profit. Our role should
> be to serve the public good.[50]

The polity likewise depends on the economy for financial support. To run effective campaigns, politicians and political parties rely on private donations. Even if money does not guarantee the outcome of an election, any candidate who hopes to win must attract significant financial support from private sources. In an editorial on the record $35 million spent by a Wall Street financier in his successful bid to become New Jersey's Democratic Senate nominee in the 2000 election, the *New York Times* noted: "The price tag for this victory now stands as a distressing symbol of a political system so driven by money that a candidate must be either extremely wealthy or extremely beholden to contributors in order to win."[51] By the beginning of the twenty-first century, staggering amounts of private money were being raised by the two major political parties in the United States to finance presidential, senatorial, and congressional electoral campaigns. Despite a ban on unregulated "soft money" contributions to the national political parties imposed by the Bipartisan Campaign Reform Act of 2002, the Republicans and Democrats had raised over a quarter of a billion dollars to finance their 2004 presidential campaigns from January 1, 2003, through April 30, 2004 ($179 million went to the Republicans, $91 million to the Democrats). The national Republicans and Democrats raised an additional $144 million and $79 million, respectively, over the same period to support 2004 Senate and House races. These huge sums exclude local party contributions and reflect fundraising a full six months prior to the November 2004 election. They also represent substantial increases in fundraising compared to the same period prior to the 2000 election.[52]

Governments also must take care to cultivate and maintain an environment hospitable to private investment. If they do not, they run the risk of being literally "downgraded" by financial markets, as happened to Detroit in the early 1990s when Moody's Investor's Services dropped the city's credit rating to noninvestment grade. Cities have little choice but to accommodate to market demands in such situations. In the words of a reporter for the *New York Times,* "A city proposes, Moody's disposes. There is no appeals court or court of last ratings resort."[53] The pursuit of the collective good is thus circumscribed by the imperatives of the private economy.

Penetration   A final way in which the dominance of the economy in the institutional balance of power is manifested is in the *penetration* of economic norms into other institutional areas. Learning takes place within the context of individualized competition for external rewards, and teaching becomes oriented toward testing. Schools rely on grading as a system of extrinsic rewards, like wages, to ensure compliance with goals. In the 1990s, many schools began forging a literal connection between academic performance and earnings: They paid students for completing assignments and for achieving high grades. In the Learning by Earning program, children earn $2 after reading a book and answering questions about it. The Renaissance Program pays students for academic achievement in the form of color-coded "Renaissance cards," which can be redeemed for free admission to school events, bookstore discounts, and discounts at local merchants. One student, who received a silver card for raising her grades to the B-minus level, responded positively to the new reward structure: "I like the competition. You want to do better than your friends. I'm shooting for a maroon card next time." Not surprisingly, local merchants also see value in the program. "It steers a lot of the kids and their families in my direction," a restaurant owner said.[54]

The penetration of the market into the schools is also reflected in their receptivity to advertising. A Georgia high school senior was suspended for wearing a Pepsi shirt to school on "Coke Day" in 1998, when schools competed for a $10,000 prize in a national contest sponsored by the soft drink company.

According to the school principal, the punishment was necessary because the student "showed disrespect for the visiting Coca-Cola team." For its part, Pepsi sent the school a check for $500. The use of students as vehicles for promoting products has not been limited to their clothing. The company "Headvertise" pays college students to wear temporary tattoos on their foreheads that convey messages for various consumer products. One student who participated in the program expressed her eagerness to do it again, despite the weird stares that she had received from her classmates, acknowledging, "It's a little embarrassing, but you get used to it."[55]

Education itself is increasingly viewed as a commodity, no different from other consumer goods. Economic terminology permeates the very language of education, as in the emphasis on the "customer-driven classroom," "accountability" conceptualized in terms of the "value added" to students in the educational production process, and the emphasis on students themselves as "products."[56] The innovation by some colleges of issuing warranties similar to a manufacturer's guarantee to accompany their diplomas offers a telling illustration of commodification. Neal Raisman, president of Rockland Community College, explained the rationale for this practice as follows: "We tell the public, 'Give us money, and we will guarantee you nothing.' I would never buy a toaster like that!"[57]

Within the polity, a "bottom-line" mentality develops. Effective politicians are those who deliver the goods. Moreover, the notion that the government would work better if it were run more like a business continues to be an article of faith among large segments of the American public. Many Americans in fact seem to prefer business leaders over public officials to perform key political functions. It is thus not surprising that successful businessman Peter Ueberroth was selected to head the "Rebuild L.A." task force established after the 1992 riot in South-Central Los Angeles, even though his prior business experience would seem to provide questionable preparation for the challenge of overcoming deep-seated social problems. In 1993, Governor Pete Wilson nominated Sanford Sigoloff, a corporate cost-cutter with no experience in educational administration, as California's superintendent of public instruction. Sigoloff's supporters evidently saw his political disinterest and lack of educational experience as pluses; these only underscored his orientation to businesslike solutions for political and educational problems. In the words of a state Senate official, "He is a technician who should be able to handle the job. The Governor made the right move in appointing someone who is not running for re-election."[58]

The family has probably been most resistant to the intrusion of economic norms. Yet even here, pressures toward penetration are apparent. Contributions to family life tend to be measured against the all-important breadwinner role, which has been extended to include women who work in the paid labor force. No corresponding movement of men into the role of homemaker has occurred. Here again, shifts in popular terminology are instructive. Husbands and wives are "partners" who "manage" the household "division of labor" in accordance with the "marriage contract." We are aware of few comparable shifts in kin-based terminology, or primary group norms, from the family to the workplace.[59]

In sum, a striking dominance of the economy in the institutional balance of power characterizes the social organization of the United States. As a result of this economic dominance, the inherent tendencies of a capitalist economy to orient the members of society toward an unrestrained pursuit of economic achievements are developed to an extreme degree. These tendencies are expressed at the cultural level in the preeminence of the competitive, individualistic pursuit of monetary success as the overriding goal—the American Dream—and in the relative de-emphasis placed on the importance of using normative means to reach this goal—anomie. The anomic nature of the American Dream and the institutional structure of American society thus mutually support and reinforce one another. In the next section, we turn to the implications of this type of social organization for crime.

SOCIAL ORGANIZATION AND CRIME

Anomie and Weak Social Institutions

Both of the core features of the social organization of the United States—culture and institutional structure—are implicated in the genesis of high levels of crime. At the cultural level, the dominant ethos of the American Dream stimulates criminal motivations and at the same time promotes a weak normative environment (anomie). At the institutional level, the dominance of the economy in the institutional balance of power undermines the vitality of non-economic institutions, reducing their capacity to control disapproved behavior and support approved behavior. And, as just explained, both culture and institutional structure are themselves interdependent. These interconnections between culture, social structure, and crime are presented schematically in Figure 4.2.

The cultural stimulation of criminal motivations derives from the distinctive content of the American Dream. Given the strong, relentless pressure for everyone to succeed, understood in terms of an inherently elusive monetary goal, people formulate wants and desires that are difficult, if not impossible, to satisfy within the confines of legally permissible behavior. This feature of the American Dream helps explain criminal behavior with an instrumental character, behavior that offers monetary rewards. This type of behavior includes white-collar offenses, street crimes such as robbery and drug dealing, and other crimes that occur as a consequence of these activities.

At the same time, the American Dream does not contain within it strong injunctions against substituting more effective, illegitimate means for less effective, legitimate means in the pursuit of monetary success. To the contrary, the distinctive cultural message accompanying the monetary success goal in the American Dream is the devaluation of all but the most technically efficient means. This anomic orientation leads not simply to high levels of crime in general but to especially violent forms of economic crime, for which the United States is known throughout the industrial world, such as mugging, carjacking, and home invasion.

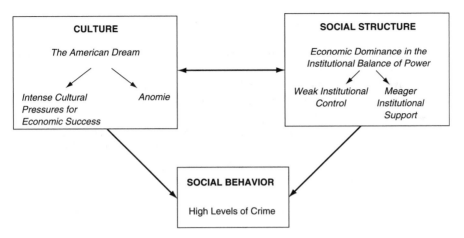

FIGURE 4.2 An Analytical Model of the Linkages Between Macrosocial Organization and Crime

Of course, the American Dream does not completely subsume culture. Other elements of culture affirm the legitimacy of legal prohibitions and the desirability of lawful behavior. In principle, these other elements of culture could counterbalance the anomic pressures emanating from the American Dream. However, the very same institutional dynamics that contribute to the pressures to "innovate" in the pursuit of economic goals also make it less likely that the anomic pressures inherent in the American Dream will in fact be counterbalanced by other cultural forces.

Prosocial cultural messages tend to be overwhelmed by the anomic tendencies of the American Dream because of the dominance of the economy in the institutional balance of power. A primary task for noneconomic institutions such as the family and schools is to inculcate beliefs, values, and commitments other than those of the marketplace. But as these noneconomic institutions are relatively devalued and forced to accommodate to economic considerations, and as they are penetrated by economic standards, they are less able to fulfill their distinctive socialization functions successfully, including the function of social control. Sociologist Robert Bellah and his colleagues have made essentially the same point in their critique of the institutional structure of contemporary American society: "Economic institutions have invaded other institutions (politics, religion, family, etc.), making it harder for them to do what they were originally intended to do."[60]

Impotent families and schools are severely handicapped in their efforts to promote allegiance to social rules, including legal prohibitions. In the absence of strong socializing influences from these noneconomic institutions, the cultural message that comes through with greatest force is the one most compatible with the logic of the economy: the competitive, individualistic, and materialistic message of the American Dream. The anomie associated with this cultural ethos thus tends to neutralize and overpower normative restraints generally, and the selection of the means for realizing *goals of any type,* not simply monetary goals, tends to be guided mainly by considerations of technical expediency.

This generalized anomie ultimately explains, in our view, the unusually high levels of gun-related violence in the United States. In the final analysis, guns are very effective tools for enforcing compliance. The American penchant for owning guns and using them reflects, in other words, a more general anomic cultural orientation, a willingness to pursue goals by any means necessary.

The basic social organization of the United States contributes to high levels of crime in another way. Institutions such as the family, schools, and the polity bear responsibility not only for socialization, and hence the internal, normative control associated with culture, but also for the more external type of social control associated with social structure. External control is achieved through the active involvement of individuals in institutional roles and through the dispensation of rewards and punishments by institutions.

Social relationships within institutions are inevitably somewhat constraining for individuals. Indeed, the very concept of institutional "roles" implies restraint. Roles consist of behavioral expectations attached to social statuses, and thus the enactment of social roles implies that an individual's behavior is governed, at least to some extent, by constraints external to the individual. However, to the degree that noneconomic institutions are relatively devalued, the attractiveness of the roles that they offer for members of society is diminished. There is, accordingly, widespread detachment from these institutions and weak institutional control.

Economic roles, in contrast, are not culturally devalued but extolled. Yet the lack of restraint associated with detachment from noneconomic institutions is not effectively counterbalanced by economic controls. Institutions vary with respect to the extent to which they impose restraints on individuals, and the nature of this variation reflects the larger culture. In American society, the economy is an institution that by design is much less constraining than other institutions. It is a free-market economy, governed by the principle of laissez-faire. Ironically, then, Americans tend to be most strongly attached to the institution with the least restraining qualities—the economy. A lack of control at the level of institutional relationships thus parallels and complements the lack of control at the cultural level of social norms.

The relative impotence of noneconomic institutions also implies that they are limited in the social support that they can offer for culturally prescribed behavior.[61] For example, the government is constrained in its capacity to mobilize resources, not only economic but also moral resources, to facilitate the pursuit of personal and collective goals. Single-parent families or those in which both parents have full-time jobs often have difficulty providing children with the emotional support and nurturance to deal with everyday misfortunes.[62] All families must rely to some extent on other institutions, usually the schools, for assistance in child-rearing. Yet poorly funded or crowded schools typically cannot supplement meager familial resources.

Finally, weak institutions invite challenge. Under conditions of extreme competitive individualism, people actively resist institutional control. Not only do they fall from the insecure grasp of powerless institutions, sometimes they deliberately, even proudly, push themselves away, and powerlessness implies reduced capacity to support as well as control. The problem of *external* control by major social institutions, then, is inseparable from the problem of the *internal* regulatory force of social norms, or anomie. Anomic societies will inevitably find it difficult and costly to exert social control over the behavior of people who feel free to use whatever means prove most effective in reaching personal goals. Hence, the very socio-cultural dynamics that make American institutions weak also enable and entitle Americans to defy institutional controls. If Americans are exceptionally resistant to social control—and therefore exceptionally vulnerable to criminal temptations—the resistance occurs because they live in a society that enshrines the unfettered pursuit of individual material success above all other values. In the United States, anomie is considered a virtue.

The Social Distribution of Crime: Gender and Race

Thus far, we have described anomic pressures that derive from the basic social organization of American society. The intensity and pervasiveness of these pressures help explain the high crime rates in the United States in comparison with those of other advanced societies. It is also important, however, to ask whether the theoretical framework we have proposed for explaining the distinctive position of the United States when considered in international perspective can also account for the social distribution of crime within the nation. We believe that the logic of our argument is compatible with observed differences in crime rates across social categories in American society. Specifically, it helps account for two of the most striking observations about the social correlates of crime: the comparatively low rates of offending for females, and the comparatively high rates of offending for African-Americans.

A wide range of evidence supports the claim that females are less involved in serious crime than are men. Official arrest statistics, victimization surveys, and self-reports of criminal activity consistently reflect this pattern.[63] An important reason for this gender differential, we suggest, is that females are much more engaged than are males in a key social institution: the family.

Women usually perform the bulk of family tasks. They typically do more of the housework than men, spend more time on childcare, and devote more time and effort to monitoring the well-being of marital relationships. Middle-aged daughters are also more likely than sons to provide services and support to aging parents. Even when women work in the paid labor force, they continue to bear primary responsibility for marriage, housework, parenthood, and kinship networks. For example, 59 percent of wives employed full-time report that their husbands do less than half of the housework, while only 14 percent of husbands say their wives do less than half of the housework.[64]

This greater engagement in family life should lead to somewhat different cultural orientations for females in comparison with males, given the general logic of our argument about the interdependency between institutional roles and culture. Women should be less likely to exhibit unqualified support for the values associated with economic achievement and more likely to balance economic values with other values consistent with familial roles. In other words, men and women should interpret the American Dream somewhat differently. The commitment to materialism and individualistic competition—values associated with the market economy—should be weaker among females than among males. On the other hand, a value preference indicating a willingness to restrain self-interest out of concern for others, which is indispensable to the enactment of familial roles, should be stronger for females than for males.

Such gender differences in value orientations have in fact been documented in the literature. Sociologists Ann Beutel and Margaret Mooney Marini report in a study of nationally representative samples of U.S. high school seniors, spanning the period from the mid-1970s to the early 1990s, that male respondents are significantly more likely than female respondents to embrace the values of a market economy: "making profits, material acquisition, and competition." On the other hand, female students are more likely to express compassion and indicate a willingness to forgo personal rewards to assist others who are in need. Similar gender differences have been observed for adult men and women in their orientations toward jobs. Women place a comparatively strong emphasis on the importance of being able to help others, and they are less likely to demonstrate a competitive orientation. In addition, females are significantly more likely than males to rate having children and getting married as an important personal goal.[65] Women, in other words, are more fully socialized into an institutional logic independent of that of the economy. As a result, we suggest that the anomic pressures of the American Dream are somewhat tempered for women, and their lesser involvement in crime is theoretically explainable.[66]

How long such institutional insulation from criminogenic pressures will last is an open question, especially given the increasing economic pressures that impinge on the family. There is no magical permanence in the tie between women and the family. Indeed, some anthropologists have claimed that the spell of the procreative and familial imperative has finally broken for large numbers of women as well as men. Managing a family and two full-time jobs imposes enormous strains on both women and men, but especially on women, and threatens the stability of marital and family bonds. Marriage and family are threatened even more by declines in manufacturing jobs, wages, and employment security associated with global economic pressures and the "deindustrialization" of the American economy. Middle- and working-class families bear the brunt of the trend toward "the second shift"—a job both in the marketplace and at home.[67] The poor, particularly the urban underclass, have been hit hardest by these structural economic shifts. Without greater insulation of the family itself from the pressures emanating from the economy, the inhibiting effects of extensive familial involvement on crime might very well diminish in the years ahead, and the crime rates of men and women could begin to converge.[68]

The institution of the family also figures importantly in the relationship between race and crime. As documented in Chapter 2, African-Americans are disproportionately involved as victims and as offenders in conventional criminal activity. Although they do not fully account for the dominance of the United States in international crime rankings, race differences in criminal offending within the nation are large and persistent. They are especially pronounced for violent crimes. Racial bias in the criminal justice system has not disappeared, but it does not explain the differential criminal involvement of African-Americans.[69] That disproportionate involvement results, we suggest, from broader cultural and structural conditions.

The explanation we offer for the "overinvolvement" of African-Americans in crime is essentially the mirror image of that we presented for the "underinvolvement" of women. We have argued that the lower level of crime among women is related to gender differences in noneconomic roles and responsibilities. Women's stronger connection with the family, in particular, insulates them to some degree from the full force of anomic cultural pressures. For a segment of the African-American community, this pattern of cultural insulation and structural engagement is reversed: Family ties are tenuous for many young black men living in U.S. inner cities, leaving them fully exposed to the promise and pitfalls of the American Dream.

Any discussion of the role of the family in the African-American community must acknowledge its durability and vitality in the face of persisting structural disadvantage. The black family survived the horrors of forced immigration to America, the brutalities of slavery, and the routine privations and frequent violence of Jim Crow segregation. Yet, what the slave system and its aftermath could not destroy is under siege by the "urban plantation" of the inner-city ghetto.[70] The family has not disappeared in inner-city communities, but the roles of men as husbands, fathers, and helpmates have been attenuated. The sources of change in the structure of the inner-city family are part of larger patterns of structural dislocation, including elevated levels of joblessness, highly concentrated poverty, and persistent racial segregation.[71] In other words, the tenuous connection between men and families in the inner city reflects an even broader institutional estrangement. Based on the logic of our explanation of crime, weakened institutional support and control are, in turn, associated with high levels of criminal involvement.

Crime in the inner city, however, is not simply a function of the alienation of young black men from the major institutions of the larger society. It is, just as important, a consequence of the assimilation of black Americans to mainstream cultural patterns, including the American Dream. Black and white Americans disagree on many things, but they are united in their commitment to the core tenets of the dominant success ideology. Large majorities of blacks and whites tell survey researchers that "the American Dream [is] alive today" and agree with the statement that it has "real meaning for you personally." Blacks are optimistic about their own and their children's mobility opportunities, and where the races do diverge somewhat in their views of success, "blacks are always the more confident." Moreover, depending on the particular survey or question, poor blacks are as likely or more likely than those in the middle class to endorse the American Dream as a highly desirable cultural prescription and as a realistic description of their personal experience.[72]

This strong affirmation of the American Dream by black Americans has had fateful consequences for the institutional life of black communities. On the one hand, without question, the promise of economic opportunity and reward has provided generations of African-Americans with the hope and determination necessary to endure oppressive and degrading social conditions. It is a wonder under the circumstances that so many have, in Hochschild's expression, remained "under the spell" of the American Dream for so long. On the other hand, African-Americans have paid a high price for their commitment to the dominant success ideology. The anomic tendencies within the Dream—the emphasis on material success by any means necessary—have inflamed the consumption desires of inner-city children and adolescents, creating a "commodity worship" that even the strongest institutions would have difficulty keeping under control. At the same time, however, the anomic ethic threatens those institutions charged with taming the self-regarding behaviors stimulated by consumption. The toll on the inner-city family has been especially heavy. In an ethnographic study of a poor neighborhood in Philadelphia, Carl Husemoller Nightingale describes the reaction of inner-city boys to their parents' unsuccessful efforts to fulfill the boys' consumption cravings:

> Boys' desires to consume conspicuously and their judgments, based on mainstream standards, about their parents' abilities as providers led to doubts about the legitimacy of the parents' control. . . . For kids, the experience of living in a poor family amid a mass culture of abundance quickly sours their attitudes toward cooperation. . . . Parents' inability to provide the basic amenities of childhood 'as seen on tv,' their occasional wishful, desperate promises to the contrary, and their kids' memories of disappointment help forge a set of cynical assumptions about other people's motives in general, a first step toward the sense that one must manipulate and hustle in order to get what one desires.[73]

Although they are felt most acutely within the family, the anomic forces of the dominant culture have invaded other inner-city institutions as well. If left unchecked, they produce with disturbing frequency the scenes of institutional collapse and personal anguish depicted in Chapter 2. The growth of illicit drug markets during the 1980s reflected and promoted the anomic climate and institutional breakdown of American inner-city communities, and contributed importantly to epidemic increases in criminal violence, particularly among adolescents and young adults. As a final illustration of the utility of our theory for understanding serious crime in the United States, we close this chapter with an assessment of how broader cultural and institutional forces were manifested in the deadly connection between illicit drugs and youth violence in the inner city.

Kids, Drugs, Guns, and Violence

As discussed in Chapter 2, rates of serious criminal violence in the United States, although chronically high by international standards, do tend to rise and fall over time. One period of increase that attracted significant public attention occurred between the mid-1980s and early 1990s. After peaking in 1980 at a rate of 10.2 per 100,000 population, the U.S. homicide rate fell to a trough of 7.9 in 1985. It then began cycling upward again, reaching another peak of 9.8 in 1991, a full 24 percent increase over the 1985 rate.[74] Robbery trends closely paralleled those for homicide, peaking at 273 robberies per 100,000 in 1991, a 31 percent increase over the 1985 rate of 208.

As sharp as these upward swings in the total rates of homicide and robbery are, they mask important subgroup differences. The homicide rate for adults aged 24 and above was relatively flat during the 1980s and early 1990s; virtually all of the growth in the total rate reflected an explosive increase in rates of youth homicide. The homicide victimization rate for 18–24-year-olds increased 102 percent between 1985 and 1993; the victimization rate for 14–17-year-olds rose 147 percent. In the mid-1980s, 14–17-year-olds had the same risk of dying from a homicide as persons aged 50 and older. By 1993, adolescents' homicide risk was nearly three times that of those 50 and older. These figures reflect the risk of homicide *victimization;* rates of homicide *offending* among teenagers and young adults went up even more.[75] Unfortunately, comparable data on age-specific trends in robbery are not available. However, robbery arrest rates for persons in their teens and early twenties, which are a rough proxy for underlying offending patterns in this age group, also increased sharply between the mid-1980s and early 1990s.[76]

The upsurge in serious violence, then, was driven by changes among youth. The increase in youth violence—more precisely for homicide, the only offense for which such descriptive data are available—occurred first in the largest cities and later in the smaller ones, was greater for males than females and African-American than white youth, and was confined to the firearm category. Levels of homicide involving knives, clubs, or no weapons remained fairly stationary during the period of increasing violence. The escalation in homicide rates, in other words, was concentrated among young African-American males in the large cities and involved the use of guns.

After peaking in the early 1990s, rates of homicide and robbery began to fall. By 2000 the total homicide and robbery rates had declined by over 40 percent from their 1991 peak levels, to 5.5 and 145 per 100,000 population, respectively. The drop in serious criminal violence mirrored the increase: It occurred first in the largest cities and spread later to the smaller ones, it was most pronounced among young African-American males, and it was concentrated in the firearm category.[77] These demographic dimensions of the recent violent crime trends do not in themselves explain the trends, but they do establish some requirements that any credible explanation must meet. Explanations emphasizing the central role of changes in urban drug markets are particularly attractive in that respect.

For one thing, such explanations are causally symmetrical: they account for both the increase and the decline in violence.[78] Rates of serious violence went up during the rise phase of the crack-cocaine epidemic and went down during the decline phase. As the crack epidemic spread in the middle to late 1980s, so did the danger around inner-city drug markets, driving up the incentive for more kids to arm themselves in an increasingly threatening environment. That environment also became a prime recruiting ground for urban street gangs. Once kids acquired guns to protect themselves from other kids, a classic arms race began, and firearm violence diffused away from the drug markets. As the crack epidemic began to abate in the early 1990s, levels of firearm violence fell as well, with some lag due to the self-perpetuating, "contagious" quality of an arms race.[79]

The focus on changes in drug markets also helps to account for the variable timing of the peaks and declines in homicide across cities. A large coastal city such as New York, for example, where crack took hold earlier and where it peaked sooner than in other cities, should have experienced a drop in its rate of homicide sooner than in other cities—and it did.[80] An additional advantage of the drug-market explanation is that it directs attention to the population groups in which the changes in homicide were concentrated: youth, not necessarily as drug users but as attractive sellers because of their reduced legal liability, and African-American youth in particular, who disproportionately participated as sellers in inner-city crack markets.

A great deal of suggestive evidence, therefore, points to inner-city crack markets as the staging ground for the rise during the 1980s of serious youth violence in the United States. Why are illicit drug markets connected to violence? By definition, trafficking in illicit commodities is illegal, which makes it difficult to make use of the police and courts to settle disputes that arise in the course of doing business. In the absence of recourse to formal dispute-resolution mechanisms, violence is used to enforce organizational discipline, secure territory and supplies from competitors, and prevent local residents from calling the police. Personal violence, then, becomes a form of "self-help" when the means of formal social control are inaccessible.[81]

What attracted many inner-city young men to an enterprise that they clearly knew carried great legal and physical risk? An ethnographic study of crack sellers concludes that selling drugs has three major attractions for inner-city youth: the promise of easy money, autonomy from the dull and confining routines of available legitimate work, and for some, addiction to the drug itself.[82] For young men with few skills and limited prospects, selling drugs is a way of securing the American Dream, and it bears undeniable similarities to other, more legitimate paths to success. "Except for the fact that it is illegal," notes one ethnographer, "selling drugs is much like selling anything else."[83] William Adler's account of the Chambers brothers, who ran a highly lucrative crack business in Detroit during the 1980s, compares their pursuit of financial gain with that of "mainstream capitalists": "Like any successful entrepreneurs, they identified a niche in the marketplace, assessed the barriers to entry, learned how to buy wholesale, mass-produce and market their product and track inventory." If the tools of their trade differed from those of legitimate businesses—they "broke knees and heads, shot people, burned houses"—their goals did not. Adler states:

> They did not reject mainstream values; rather they embraced them in the only way they could. In yearning and looking and groping for a way out, the Chambers did what most Americans would have said was the right thing to do had they not sold drugs: they strove for financial success. Indeed, their story should frighten not because it shows what made them different, but rather what made them so common.[84]

As the crack epidemic crested and declined, the illegitimate opportunities for "making it" through drug selling also diminished. Fortunately, opportunities within the legitimate economy began to grow at the same time, as the United States entered a period of record economic expansion in the 1990s. The role of opportunities in the legitimate labor market interacts in complex ways with changes in the illicit opportunity-structure of distressed urban communities. The availability of low-wage jobs in the secondary labor market is particularly relevant when illicit markets and the employment opportunities they offer are shrinking. If young people resort to criminal activity in the absence of legitimate opportunities for success, according to traditional anomie theory, they also can turn to legitimate jobs in response to dwindling opportunities for illegitimate work. Economist Richard Freeman's analyses of youth employment surveys indicate that a sizable fraction of inner-city young men engage in both legal and illegal activity at the same time, moving back and forth from one to the other as opportunity permits.[85]

There may be much to criticize about the low-end "go nowhere" jobs produced during the economic expansion of the 1990s, but they do employ teenagers—they are the only kinds of jobs for which the great majority of teenagers are qualified—and they do reduce the risk of teenagers becoming crime victims or offenders. Kids are far less likely to kill or be killed when working in a fast-food restaurant or supermarket than when selling crack on the corner outside. These effects, however, are inherently short-term, not only because of the cyclical character of legitimate employment opportunities, but also because jobs in the secondary labor market are not, by themselves, a strong foundation for the kind of long-term integration in the economic, social, and *moral* life of a community that is necessary to permanently reduce the economic attractions of drug selling and other forms of crime.

The Social Response to Crime

We made the point in Chapter 2 that the United States is exceptional compared with other developed nations not only in its high rates of serious crime but in the *combination* of high crime and harsh punishment. Thus far in the present chapter, we have argued that fundamental features of social organization – the society's culture and institutional structure – produce the relatively high levels of crime. To conclude this chapter, we advance the thesis that the U.S. *response* to crime is also the result of many of the same cultural and social conditions that give rise to high crime rates.

At the cultural level, punishment in the United States is guided by an anomic inattention to means relative to the goal of crime reduction through the incapacitation of "common" criminals, up to and including execution. At the structural level, the comparative weakness of the polity and family leads to a striking lack of institutional support for incarcerated offenders and ex-prisoners. Other developed nations rely much less on prisons and much more on day fines and formal and informal community sanctions for both punishing and rehabilitating criminals.[86] Community-based sanctions presuppose strong concerns about the social reintegration of persons who violate the law, including the maintenance of family bonds and the provision of social services. Sutton has argued that developed nations with "corporatist" labor-market arrangements, in which free-market arrangements are tempered by paid parental leave, family allowances, universal health care, and related provisions, "discourage high imprisonment rates ... as part of a broader orientation to inclusive and egalitarian forms of social policy."[87] By contrast, the United States depends more heavily on incarceration as the punishment of first and last resort, and ex-prisoners are left to fend for themselves under the very same conditions that led to their crimes in the first place.

If punishment by any means necessary typifies the U.S. response to crime, what accounts for the comparatively light punishment of white-collar criminals? Conflict theories have a straightforward answer to this question: The distribution of punishment mirrors the distribution of wealth and power in the society. As such, we should expect to observe stronger punishment of the powerless than the powerful.[88] This explanation is persuasive as far as it goes, but there is an institutional dimension to class differences in punishment as well.

By most definitions, white-collar crime is committed in the course of doing business. Often, such offenses represent incremental steps beyond lawful business practices. Where is the line, for example, between hyperbole in advertising and fraudulent deception? Because much white-collar crime so closely resembles the practice of business itself in a competitive, free-market context, it is often difficult to conceive of white-collar crime as "crime," a point we made in Chapter 2. This is part of the reason for the low level of criminalization of harmful business practices. It also helps to explain the meager sanctions applied to white-collar offending. To punish white-collar crime too harshly risks calling into question the very practices that constitute "doing business" in a free-market economy. In the punishment realm, the dominance of the economy manifests itself in sanctions the form and magnitude of which affirm the legitimacy of free-market arrangements. The preponderance of civil over criminal penalties for legal transgressions and the use of fines rather than imprisonment when criminal sanctions are imposed seem to "make sense" in the case of white-collar crime; they represent yet another kind of monetary transaction that is simply part of the cost of doing business.

This prompts a final question for our analysis of crime in American society. If crime and the response to crime are firmly rooted in social organization, what kinds of cultural and social changes are required to change the status quo? In the next chapter, we explain how conventional crime control strategies from both ends of the ideological spectrum are seriously flawed precisely because they reinforce rather than challenge the sociocultural foundations of crime. We address the limitations of those strategies and propose alternative directions for change that are consistent with our explanation of the anomic consequences of the American Dream.

NOTES

1. Hacker (1992, p. 29).

2. The Quotations Page, http://www.quotationspage.com/quotes/Ronald_Reagan/11.

3. Wicker (1991, pp. 686–687).

4. Heilbroner (1991, pp. 538–539).

5. In our analysis of the value foundations of the American Dream, we rely heavily on Marco Orru's (1990) excellent exegesis of Merton's theory. Characterizations of this cultural ethos that are very similar to ours also can be found in studies of the "success theme" in American literature cited in Chapter 1. See Hearn (1977) and Long (1985).

6. The reference to the "fetishism of money" is from Taylor, Walton, and Young's (1973, p. 94) insightful discussion of Merton's theory of anomie.

7. Hochschild (1995, p. xi). Turner and Musick (1985) similarly emphasize the degree of consensus over "basic values" in contemporary American society.

8. Orru (1990, p. 234).

9. See in this regard Gouldner's (1970, p. 65) arguments concerning the tendency for "bourgeois utilitarian culture," of which American culture is a prime example, to place a "great stress upon winning or losing, upon success or failure as such."

10. Bellah et al. (1985, p. 142).

11. Derber (1992, 1996) identifies an unrestrained and a degraded individualism as the primary cause of a "wilding epidemic" in America. He maintains that this epidemic is ultimately responsible for both criminal behavior and legal, egoistic behavior (for example, careerists who betray colleagues to advance their own careers). Whereas Derber emphasizes the degeneration of the social order as the source of crime, which is reflected in his use of the metaphor of societal "illness," our perspective locates the causes of crime in the *normal* operations of the social system.

12. The first quotation is from Merton (1968, p. 190); the second is from Orru (1990, p. 235). See Schwartz (1994b, pp. 55–113) for further discussion of the tendency for economic success to become "the measure of all things" in the professions, sports, and other areas of American life.

13. The references to "no final stopping point" and "never-ending achievement" are from Merton (1968, p. 190) and Passas (1990, p. 159), respectively.

14. The African-American youth is quoted in Wilkerson (1992, p. B7). The quotation on the role of the media is from O'Connor (1993).

15. Merton (1968, p. 189).

16. The quotation is from Bassis, Gelles, and Levine (1991, p. 142). Our discussion of institutions draws heavily on this source. We present a formal analysis of the various uses of the concept of "institutions" in criminological theory in Messner and Rosenfeld (2004). See also Bellah et al. (1991, Ch. 1 and App.).

17. Parsons (1964, p. 239).

18. See Berger (1963, pp. 87–91).

19. Our discussion of the needs fulfilled by institutions is based on Parsons's (1951) classic description of the functional requisites of social systems. Parsons identifies a fourth system need, the need to "integrate" the system around its core value

orientations, and he locates the legal system within this functional realm. We follow the more common practice of treating the legal system, specifically criminal justice organizations and processes, as part of the political system. The "functionalism" associated with Parsons has been harshly criticized in the sociological literature. A good review of the important controversies is provided by Downes and Rock (1982), who observe that critics of functionalism often attack absurdly "vulgarized" formulations of the perspective (p. 75). We concur with these authors' general conclusion that although functionalists may have "overplayed their hand, . . . at least they are playing the right sort of game" (p. 93).

20. Bassis, Gelles, and Levine (1991, p. 142).

21. Lasch (1977).

22. See Johnson, De Li, Larson, and McCullough (2000) on the relationship between religion and delinquency. Surette (1992) provides a good overview of research on the mass media, crime, and justice. Much research on crime and the mass media occurs within a "social constructionist" theoretical tradition. See Potter and Kappeler (1998) for examples.

23. Cited in MacLeod (1987, pp. 11–14).

24. Babbie (1992, p. 41).

25. The classic discussion of basic value patterns governing the orientation of actors in social situations is Parsons (1951).

26. See Blau and Blau (1982) and Messner and Golden (1992) for arguments about the relationship between ascriptive inequality and criminal violence. The premise that deviance can be understood with reference to the normal workings of societal institutions is characteristic of the general functionalist approach in sociology. See, in particular, Wright and Hilbert (1980).

27. Passas (1990, pp. 158–159). Polanyi ([1944] 1957) argues convincingly that this orientation of economic activity around the self-interested pursuit of profit and gain is not an inevitable, "natural" feature of the human species. Rather, it is unique to capitalist societies.

28. Elkins (1968, p. 43).

29. Elkins (1968, p. 33).

30. Elkins (1968, p. 43n).

31. Heilbroner (1991, pp. 539–540).

32. See Lane (1971).

33. Also consistent with our general argument, Currie observes that "the United States has long been the most market-dominated of Western industrial countries, the one with the least developed alternatives to the values and institutions of the market." Both quotations are from Currie (1991, p. 255). For a classic discussion of the tendency for markets to dominate other institutions in capitalist societies, and the dangers of this tendency, see Polanyi ([1944] 1957).

34. Waldman and Springen (1992, p. 81).

35. The quotations are from Beck (1993, p. 68). The earnings rankings and figures for child-care workers and animal caretakers are from the Bureau of Labor Statistics, retrieved online at http://stats.bls.gov/ncs/ocs/sp/ncar0002.pdf.

36. Adler (1983, p. 131).

37. The statistics on voting for 1996 and 2000 are from the U.S. Census Bureau, retrieved online at http://www.census.gov/population/socdemo/voting/tabA-4.pdf. The statistics for 2004 are from http://www.census.gov/population/sociodemo/voting/cps2004/tab01.xls. For rates of participation in U.S. presidential elections since 1928, see *New York Times* (1998, p. 115). The cross-national comparison of national voter turnout is from Taylor and Jodice (1983, pp. 76–78).

38. Will (1992).

39. See Edsall (1992, p. 10).

40. Authors' calculations from the 2002 GSS.

41. Edsall (1992, p. 9); *New York Times* (1994).

42. See Presser (2003).

43. Figure 4.1 is based on data from The Clearinghouse on International Developments in Child, Youth, and Family Policies at Columbia University. The data have been retrieved from Table 1.11 at http://www.childpolicyintl.org. Note that Figure 4.1 allows for only rough comparisons because nations differ in the level of compensation and in specific features of mandated leaves. For example, the duration of leaves in France varies according to the birth order. See the original source for details.

44. The reference to Italian mothers' "birthright" is from Bohlen (1996, p. 1), who also describes family leave and related support policies in other European nations. Gornick and Meyers (2003) offer a comprehensive description of family support policies in other nations and suggestions for policy changes in the United States.

45. Adler (1983, p. 132). Japanese businesses also place a higher priority on providing jobs for their employees than on customer satisfaction and shareholder interests. As Friedman (1996, p. E15) explains, "The Japanese understand that a job gives dignity and stability to people's lives and pays off in much greater social harmony. Just walk the streets of Tokyo: few homeless sleeping on grates, no muggers lurking in the shadows."

46. See Wilson (1987, 1996).

47. Thomson (1992).

48. The example of the school maintaining its gym with financial support from a local supermarket is reported in Quindlen (2004). The Field Trip Faculty is described in an editorial from the *Philadelphia Inquirer* (2004).

49. Strosnider (1997, p. A31).

50. Press and Washburn (2000).

51. The editorial comment on the "distressing symbol" of big-money campaigns is from *New York Times* (2000).

52. The dollar amounts are from a news release issued by the Federal Election Commission on May 26, 2004. Source: http://www.fec.gov/press/press2004/20040526party/20040526ptystat.html. Accessed July 27, 2004.

53. *New York Times* (1992, p. C1).

54. The Learning by Earning program was initiated in Georgia by then-Speaker of the U.S. House of Representatives Newt Gingrich and subsequently implemented on a national scale (*Albany Times-Union*, 1995, p. A6). The Renaissance Program was created by Jostens, Inc., a company that makes school rings and yearbooks. As of the mid-1990s, 3500 schools participated in the program nationwide (quoted material from Volland, 1994, p. 2B; see also Tetzeli [1992, p. 80]).

55. The suspension of a student on Coke Day is reported in Hiaasen (1998). The company "Headvertise" is discussed in O'Keefe (2003).

56. For commentary on the notion of the "customer-driven classroom," see *The Teaching Professor* (1994). The references to "accountability" and "value-added" education are from Kozol (1992, p. 277). See also Kozol's (1991) discussion of the state of American public education, and Bellah et al.'s (1991, p. 170) critique of the idea of an "education industry."

57. Hancock (1995, p. 44).

58. Celis (1993, p. A12). The trend toward choosing successful business leaders to head public education systems accelerated during the 1990s. In May 2000, for example, Harold O. Levy, a corporate lawyer, was appointed superintendent of the New York City school system, the largest in the nation (Lewin, 2000).

59. For a particularly insightful discussion of the penetration of market-based norms and metaphors into noneconomic realms of social life, see Schwartz (1994a, 1994b). Schwartz (1994b, p. 361) observes that "along with the language of the market, people have increasingly adopted the practices of the market." An example of the application of kin-based terminology to the marketplace, brought to our attention by an undergraduate student, is that of a "parent corporation."

60. Bellah et al. (1991, p. 291). Similar arguments about the consequences of economic "invasion" for other social institutions can be found in Currie (1991), Schwartz (1994b), and Wolfe (1989).

61. On the role of "social support" in limiting crime, see Cullen and Wright (1997).

62. See Snyder and Patterson (1987) for a discussion of research on parenting and juvenile delinquency.

63. Steffensmeier and Allan (1995). The overrepresentation of males is not always observed for minor forms of offending in self-report studies. When serious offenses are considered, however, the results of self-report studies are consistent with those based on other data sources.

64. Based on authors' calculations from the 1996 GSS. Compared with males, female respondents in the 1998 GSS reported spending more time with parents, siblings, and other relations. See Thompson and Walker (1991) for a review of the literature on gender differences in family involvement.

65. The study of value orientations of high school students is reported in Beutel and Marini (1995). The quotation appears on page 438. These authors also summarize research on gender differences in value orientations for adults. The reference to the greater emphasis on the goal of childbearing and getting married for females is based on responses in the 2002 GSS (authors' calculations).

66. Our explanation of gender differences in offending in the contemporary United States is consistent with observations for the mid-nineteenth century made by the classic social analyst, Alexis de Tocqueville. As Barry Schwartz (1994b, pp. 222–223) explains, Tocqueville believed that women's extensive involvement in the family served as "the counterweight to the pursuit of selfish interests in the marketplace."

67. The reference to the "second shift" is from Hochschild (1989). Harris (1981, pp. 76–97) discusses declining commitment to family and parenting. See Harrison and Bluestone (1988, p. 138) for a discussion of how deindustrialization is "wreaking havoc with the American dream."

68. Gender convergence need not lead to an increase in crime rates. The logic of our argument implies that greater engagement of men in familial roles should reduce their exposure to anomic pressures and lower their criminal involvement to a level more similar to that of women, thereby reducing overall rates of crime. We discuss the importance for crime control of revitalizing the family in Chapter 5.

69. See Tonry (1995) for a summary of race differences in levels and patterns of criminal offending and an insightful discussion of the role of race in crime control policy and practice in the United States.

70. The term "urban plantation" is from Staples (1987). See Gutman (1976) for a compelling account of the efforts by black Americans after the Civil War to reunite families that had been split apart during slavery. Good discussions of the contemporary black family and the precarious position of inner-city families can be found in Cherlin (1992, pp. 91–123), Hacker (1992, pp. 67–92), and Wilson (1987, 1996).

71. See Massey and Denton (1993) for a penetrating treatment of racial segregation and the development of the ghetto underclass.

72. Jennifer Hochschild's *Facing Up to the American Dream* (1995) provides an exhaustive summary of survey research on blacks' and whites' perceptions and beliefs regarding the dominant success ideology. The quoted material in this paragraph is from pages 56–57 of Hochschild's book; see pages 72–88 for evidence on class differences in African-Americans' attitudes toward the American Dream.

73. Nightingale (1993, pp. 148, 160). Nightingale uses the term "commodity worship" to describe the acute consumption pressures experienced by some inner-city adolescents (see pp. 143–165).

74. These figures, which are from the FBI's Uniform Crime Reports, differ slightly from the vital statistics data presented in Figure 2.3. Except where noted otherwise, the material in this section is drawn from Blumstein and Rosenfeld (1998, 1999).

75. The age-specific homicide figures are based on SHR data reported by the BJS at http://www.ojp.usdoj.gov/bjs/homicide.

76. See Blumstein and Rosenfeld (1999, p. 150) for a discussion of the validity of arrest data as an indicator of criminal offending.

77. For discussions of the dimensions and hypothesized sources of the decline in criminal violence during the 1990s, see Blumstein and Wallman (2000); Rosenfeld (2004b). The crime figures in the text are from the latter source.

78. Material in this section and below is drawn from Blumstein and Rosenfeld (1998, pp. 1209–1212).

79. For evidence that urban robbery rates increased as a function of growth in crack involvement, see Baumer et al. (1998). Sheley and Wright (1995) provide survey evidence connecting drug-market activity with firearm possession by inner-city adolescents. Cork (1999) presents evidence that the rise and fall of drug-market activity in U.S. cities preceded the corresponding increase and decline of youth firearm violence. For a general statement linking the rise in youth firearm violence to changes in urban drug markets, see Blumstein (1995).

80. Using urinalysis data to document the drug use of persons arrested for misdemeanors and felonies in U.S. cities, Golub and Johnson (1997) show that the upsurge, peak, and decline in cocaine use by criminal suspects tended to occur first in the larger coastal cities and one or more years later in the smaller cities.

81. Black (1984); see also Sullivan (1988, p. 240).

82. Jacobs (1999, pp. 26–42).

83. Sullivan (1988, p. 239).

84. Adler (1995, pp. 6–7).

85. Freeman (1996).

86. On the use of day fines as an alternative to imprisonment in European nations, see Reichel (2002, pp. 269-270).

87. Sutton (2004, p. 184).

88. See Chambliss and Seidman (1971); Vold, Bernard, and Snipes (2002, pp. 240-242).

5

Strengthening Social Institutions and Rethinking the American Dream

> There is a hollowness at the core of a society if its members share
> no common purpose, no mutual goals, no joint vision—nothing
> to believe in except self-aggrandizement.
> (MARIAN WRIGHT EDELMAN)[1]

> In Dreams Begin Responsibilities
> (DELMORE SCHWARTZ)[2]

In 1929, James Truslow Adams, historian of the American Dream, called attention to the alarming crime problem in the United States. Adams believed that the task of reducing crime in America was urgent and that it would require alterations in basic social and cultural patterns. He also recognized the role of human agency in social change and the importance of leadership at the highest levels in mobilizing the resources necessary to reform the "very foundations" of American life. In his view, nothing less than American democracy itself was at stake. "We must rule or be ruled," he wrote, because unless the crime problem is brought under control, social order will sooner or later give way to chaos, opening the way for "the dictator who inevitably 'saves society' when social insubordination and disintegration have become intolerable."[3]

Adams directed his message for change, published in an essay on law observance, to Herbert Hoover. It is easy in retrospect to dismiss as futile his effort to educate President Hoover on the nature of the crime problem.

However, Adams was well aware of the president's public policy limitations. Hoover may not have understood the "magnitude and the causes of the danger which we face," but at least he acknowledged that a crime problem existed. By contrast, his predecessor, Calvin Coolidge, "never troubled himself over the rising tide of crime and lawlessness, beyond seeing to it that Mrs. Coolidge was accompanied on her shopping by an armed protector."[4]

Several important lessons remain in Adams's attempts to educate the president and the public about crime. If Adams exaggerated the specter of social collapse and dictatorship, he recognized the genuine vulnerability of democratic rights and freedoms to demagogic appeals for "law and order." He also understood the importance of establishing a supportive intellectual climate for effective political leadership and public action. Hoover's moral appeals to citizens to do their "duty" by obeying the Eighteenth Amendment prohibition against the manufacture, sale, or transportation of intoxicating liquors were ineffective, in Adams's view, because they reflected a shallow appreciation of the American crime problem.

> The American problem, though complicated by Prohibition, lies far
> deeper; and it is the lack of understanding as to what the problem is that
> so greatly diminishes the force of Mr. Hoover's appeal to us as citizens
> anxious to do our duty toward society.[5]

Adams also contributes very important insights regarding the causes of crime and prospects for crime policy in America. His message is organized around two themes that are central to our arguments. First, the roots of the American crime problem lie deep within our cultural and institutional history. "Lawlessness," by which Adams meant a generalized disrespect for law as such, is part of the American heritage. Prohibition may have contributed to the problem, he wrote in a 1928 *Atlantic* article titled "Our Lawless Heritage,"

> but it is operating upon a population already the most lawless in spirit of
> any in the great modern civilized countries. Lawlessness has been and is
> one of the most distinctive American traits. . . . It is needless to say that
> we are not going to be able to shed this heritage quickly or easily.[6]

Second, because high rates of crime are neither recent nor ephemeral characteristics of American society, responses to crime must be equally fundamental if they are to be effective. According to Adams, the "spirit" of lawlessness, very similar to what we have termed the ethic of anomie, will give way only when the preconditions for respect for law have been established. These include knowledge of the nature and limits of law on the part of lawmakers and the public, and the impartial application of legal sanctions against "millionaires" and "highly placed officials in Washington," as well as against the "ordinary criminal." Most important, the American spirit of lawlessness will not abate "until the ideal of quickly accumulated wealth, by any means whatever, is made subordinate to the ideal of private and public virtue."[7]

Adams does not describe in detail how these changes are to come about, in particular how virtue would overcome the goal of material accumulation, except to propose that the president has, if he would only seize it, an opportunity to exercise essential moral leadership. Although directed at Herbert Hoover in 1929, Adams's call for moral "regeneration" continues to be relevant to present-day political and cultural conditions, as the quotation from Marian Wright Edelman at the beginning of this chapter suggests. If the president, in Adams's words,

> will undertake to show the people what underlies their problem, and assume the leadership in a crusade to reform the very foundations of their life, . . . then he will prove the leader for whom America waits, and patriotism and nobility may again rise above efficiency and wealth. By that path only can America regain respect for law and for herself. . . . America can be saved, but it must be by regeneration, not by efficiency.[8]

We share Adams's belief that significant reductions in crime in the United States will require fundamental changes in the social and cultural order. If our diagnosis of the problem is correct—if high levels of crime derive from the very organization of American society—the logical solution is social reorganization. This will entail, in our view, both institutional reform and cultural regeneration. Before sketching the kinds of institutional and cultural changes that might reduce crime rates, however, it is important first to consider conventional approaches to crime control and their limitations.

CONVENTIONAL STRATEGIES
FOR CRIME CONTROL

The point of departure for this discussion is current policy and proposals for alternative policies, championed by what we will call the "conservative" and "liberal" political camps. Current policy, informed largely by conservative views, has not resulted in levels of serious crime comparable to those in other advanced nations. However, proposals from the liberal camp to complement conservative "get tough" strategies with social reforms to expand opportunities for those "locked out" of the American Dream have not been much more successful. We suggest that both these approaches fail because both conservative and liberal strategies reinforce the very qualities of American culture that lead to high rates of crime in the first place.

The Conservative Camp: The War on Crime

Conservative crime control policies are draped explicitly in the metaphors of war. We have declared war on crime and on drugs, which are presumed to promote crime. Criminals, according to this view, have taken the streets, blocks, and sometimes entire neighborhoods from law-abiding citizens. Crime control policy functions to recapture the streets from criminals to make them safe for the rest of us, through a range of initiatives encompassing law enforcement, criminal prosecution, court decisions, and sanctions policy.

Let us summarize briefly the conservative scenario for successful crime control. The police will act swiftly to remove criminals from the streets, prosecutors will vigorously bring their cases to court without plea-bargaining them to charges carrying lesser penalties, judges and juries will have less discretion in determining the penalties imposed (for example, "three strikes" laws that mandate extended prison sentences for three-time offenders), and more criminals will serve longer sentences for their crimes. Corrections officials will thus keep offenders in prison for longer periods of time, both because criminal offenders are serving longer sentences and because officials will have less discretion in granting them parole. The cumulative effects of these "get tough" actions will be lower crime rates brought about by increases both in the deterrent effects of punishment and in what criminologists term the "incapacitation effects" of imprisonment. With respect to deterrence, stiffer penalties will raise the costs of crime, thereby dissuading potential offenders from committing their first crimes and convincing previous offenders that it is too costly to repeat their misdeeds. The simple logic of incapacitation is that offenders who are in prison will be unable to commit crimes against the innocent public.

Conservatives have been successful in influencing crime control policies over the course of recent decades. For the 24-year period between 1968 and 1992, the White House was occupied for all but four years by Republican presidents who proudly proclaimed their credentials as "law and order" advocates. Republican control over the presidency resulted in the nomination of conservative justices to the Supreme Court and conservative judges to the federal judiciary, and it facilitated legislative changes consistent with the conservative agenda on crime control. That agenda remained intact when the Democrats regained control of the White House for eight years beginning in 1992, to be followed again by a Republican administration. Among the most important of the conservative policy initiatives implemented during this era was the widespread adoption during the 1980s of mandatory-minimum sentencing laws.

Mandatory-Minimum Sentencing and the Drug War   Mandatory-minimum sentencing laws specify the minimum sentence for crimes and, in principle, prohibit courts and correctional agencies from modifying them. Such sentencing policy intends to increase both the certainty and the severity of punishment for persons convicted of the most serious crimes. Mandatory-minimum sentencing has been applied with special force to drug trafficking, resulting in extraordinary increases in the incarceration rates of drug offenders. Data from the National Corrections Reporting Program (NCRP) indicate that over half (52 percent) of the increase in prison admissions during the 1980s resulted from drug offenses. According to a leading criminal justice policy analyst, the use of mandatory-minimum sentencing in the war on drugs "elevated the severity of punishment for drug sales to a level comparable to that for homicide."[9]

The policies associated with the war on crime and drugs have had only limited success. We are not aware of any evidence showing that the war on drugs is responsible for declines in rates of drug abuse in the United States. The vast expansion in imprisonment, as we argued in Chapter 2, undoubtedly has resulted in some crime suppression, although how much remains a matter of debate.[10] Rates of serious crime in America have fluctuated over time, sometimes increasing and sometimes decreasing, but they have remained at very high levels despite the implementation of a host of conservative policies. Moreover, Americans do not perceive themselves to be safer than in the past. As we documented in Chapter 2, fear of crime and preoccupation with personal safety are stark realities in many parts of the nation, especially in the more disadvantaged neighborhoods of large cities.

The Expansion of Punitive Social Control   The war on crime has achieved one noteworthy victory, suggested in our discussion of mandatory-minimum sentencing, although it is surely a Pyrrhic one: Incarceration levels have soared. Over two million Americans are incarcerated. As of midyear 2002, 1,355,748 persons were serving time in state and federal prisons, and another 665,475 were in local jails, an incarceration rate of 702 inmates per 100,000 population. About 15 years earlier, in 1985, 744,208 persons were held in jail or prison, an incarceration rate of 313 per 100,000 population.[11] The rapid escalation of incarceration—a doubling in the number of inmates in under 20 years—has been expensive, especially at the state and local level where the vast majority of prison and jail inmates are housed. For example, state governments spent $8.3 million on corrections in 1985; by 1999 those expenditures had more than tripled to $30.8 million.[12]

The extraordinary increase in the population of prisons and jails is only part of a larger expansion of formal, punitive social control in the United States. As of the end of 2002, 6.7 million Americans, 3.1 percent of all adults, were under some form of correctional sanction. Roughly 2 million were in prison or jail, and the remaining 4.7 million were under supervision in the community (about 4 million on probation and 0.7 million on parole). Between 1985 and 2002, the number of adults under some form of correctional sanction in the United States increased by 123 percent.[13]

As noted in Chapter 1, African-Americans currently are subject to levels of punitive social control that are much higher than those for the population as a whole. African-Americans have been hit hard by the war against crime— and especially by the war against drugs. In his presidential address to the American Society of Criminology in the early 1990s, Alfred Blumstein characterized rising levels of arrest and incarceration of black Americans as nothing less than

> a major assault on the black community. One can be reasonably confident that if a similar assault was affecting the white community, there would be a strong and effective effort to change either the laws or the enforcement policy.[14]

Whether or not black Americans have been targeted explicitly, disturbing parallels exist between the massive expansion in formal social control during the 1980s and 1990s and the infamous "Black Codes" of the post–Civil War South. Most of the Southern states passed such vagrancy laws, allowing for the arrest of unemployed and "idle" blacks.[15] Although the intent of such policies is to control disruptive behavior, it is not clear that the aggressive sanctions policies of the last few decades have reduced offending among blacks. Crime rates fell during the late 1990s, when prison populations were increasing, but crime rates rose during the late 1980s and early 1990s, when prison populations were also increasing. Of course, crime rates may have risen even more dramatically in the 1980s or fallen less dramatically in the 1990s were it not for the expansion in incarceration. But incarceration and other forms of correctional control are, at best, a blunt instrument for purposes of crime reduction. Moreover, as we pointed out in Chapter 2, imprisonment may actually be ineffective in reducing criminality, even if it suppresses officially recorded crime through the quarantining of criminal offenders.[16]

Unintended Consequences of Expanded Punitive Control   Not only has the extension of the reach of the criminal justice system failed to bring American crime rates into line with those of most other advanced societies; it also tends to undermine the capacity of the system to realize an equally important objective: justice. Excessive caseloads put pressure on the major participants in the adjudication process—district attorneys, defense lawyers (especially public defenders), and judges—to dispense with cases quickly. A preoccupation with efficiency rather than with the rights of criminal defendants results.[17] A concern with the simple management of large numbers of cases also pervades the correctional system. Indeed, criminologists Malcolm Feeley and Jonathan Simon have argued that a new way of perceiving the very functions of criminal sanctions has become dominant in criminology and criminal justice. According to this "new penology," the focus of corrections has shifted away from a concern with administering levels of punishment that individuals deserve, or a concern with rehabilitating these offenders, to a preoccupation with more efficient "risk management" of dangerous populations.[18]

The unfortunate and unintended consequences of the war on crime, however, extend far beyond the criminal justice system itself. Crackdowns on crime are directed at those populations considered to be most dangerous to society. This implies that minority groups will be affected disproportionately by these efforts. As we have seen, this has been precisely the case for black Americans, many of whom quite understandably resent the differential treatment imposed on them by vigorous law enforcement efforts. It should come as little surprise, therefore, that police-citizen confrontations involving minority group members are likely to be filled with tension and hostility and that they can ignite episodes of collective disorder.

In addition, given the greater criminal involvement of males in comparison with females, and of young males in particular, extremely high levels of incarceration can have devastating implications for the sex ratio of a community and, in turn, for family relations. The large-scale removal of young males from the general population depletes the supply of potential marriage partners for young females. In so doing, expansive incarceration policies impede the formation of traditional families and thereby encourage, indirectly, higher rates of households headed by females and of illegitimacy—precisely the types of family conditions that have been linked with high rates of crime.[19] In short, the war on crime has failed to secure a safe environment, and in some ways it has exacerbated the very problem that it is supposed to solve.

The limitations of conservative crime control policies reflect the warfare mentality that provides their justification. This is why it is so politically dangerous to call for an end to current policy, even for those who are willing to acknowledge its limitations. It appears defeatist to advocate limits on the costs of criminal sanctions, or on the proportion of the population it is reasonable or desirable to place under correctional control, when crime control is imbued with the metaphors of war. A former official in the current drug war is said to have compared the underlying logic of the campaign with the tale of Humpty Dumpty:

> When all the King's horses and all the King's men couldn't put Humpty together again, the response was merely to double the number of horses and men, rather than to recognize at some point the futility of the effort.[20]

However, reports of violent conflict from the "battle zones" of American cities suggest that the war on crime is more than just a rhetorical device: It is a classic instance of the sociological self-fulfilling prophecy. It begins with a definition of the situation that likens the crime problem to war. The war on crime, in turn, reinforces the cultural and social arrangements that produce warlike conditions in the society. The response is to intensify the war on crime. An alternative response would be to change the initial definition of crime as "war" and criminals as "enemies." Yet this approach to crime control, taken by the liberal camp, also ends up reproducing social and cultural conditions conducive to crime.

The Liberal Camp: The War on Poverty and on Inequality of Opportunity

In contrast to conservative crackdowns on criminals, the liberal approach to crime control emphasizes correctional policies and broader social reforms intended to expand opportunities for those "locked out" of the American Dream. This approach is based on the premise that the poor and disadvantaged want to conform to the law and that they commit crimes only when doing so is necessary to achieve goals that cannot be achieved through conformity. Providing access to the legitimate means of success for those who lack opportunities can thus lessen the temptations for crime. For those who have already become enmeshed in the criminal justice system, liberals call for rehabilitation and reform, with a heavy emphasis on training and skill development to allow offenders to compete more effectively for jobs upon reentry into society.

Liberals, like conservatives, have enjoyed some notable successes in getting their policies implemented. The War on Poverty during the 1960s provides a good example of liberal strategies for general social reform. Many of the programs associated with this initiative were justified with explicit reference to crime reduction. Perhaps the most famous of these was the Mobilization for Youth program, which sought to reduce crime and delinquency in a depressed area of Manhattan by expanding educational and employment opportunities. This program was organized in part by Richard Cloward, one of the leading figures associated with the anomie perspective on crime and delinquency.[21]

Effects of Liberal Policies on Crime Rates   Little evidence suggests that the liberal strategies, including the Mobilization for Youth program, have been any more effective than the conservative approaches in substantially reducing levels of crime.[22] Crime rates increased markedly during the height of liberal social reform in the 1960s and early 1970s. Some liberal advocates have argued that their approach was never really tried, that the War on Poverty was underfunded, that it was more image than reality, or that it was quickly overwhelmed by other issues, such as the Vietnam War. Typical of this view is Ruth Sidel's comment that

> The War on Poverty was woefully inadequate to reverse the damage that was done, particularly to blacks, in our society; and no sooner did it get started than Vietnam, inflation, and the Nixon administration had begun to subvert it.[23]

However, the fact is that poverty rates in the United States did decline during the 1960s and most of the 1970s. Unless official poverty rates are rejected as grossly invalid indicators of impediments to economic opportunity, then, based on the liberal view, some relief from serious crime should have coincided with the realization of genuine social reform.[24]

We may question the effectiveness of the liberal approach to crime control for additional reasons. First, it is difficult to see how the liberal explanation of crime and the policies based on it would apply to the crimes committed by persons at the top of the opportunity structure, crimes that are far from rare and that are very costly to society. Second, although the poor disproportionately commit certain forms of serious crime, crime rates do not uniformly rise with increases in poverty, unemployment, or other indicators of economic deprivation. In fact, the opposite is the case for certain historical periods.

Crime rates fell during the Great Depression of the 1930s and rose markedly during the prosperous 1960s. Crime rates declined during the mid-1970s and then again during the early 1980s, but in both instances the reductions coincided with periods of economic recession. In contrast, crime rates dropped during sustained economic growth and low unemployment during the mid- to late 1990s. A full assessment of changes in levels of serious crime must, of course, encompass a wide range of causal factors in addition to economic opportunities, such as changes in the age composition of the population and in the routine activities that make people and property more or less vulnerable or attractive targets for crime.[25] Even so, the historical evidence fails to support the proposition that reductions in crime follow in any simple, direct manner from an expansion of economic opportunities.

The liberal approach to crime control fails, we suggest, due to an incomplete understanding of the social sources of crime in American society. Liberals are aware of the feeble institutional infrastructures to be found in many impoverished communities and neighborhoods, and they recognize the devastating implications of such structural conditions for efforts at crime control. However, liberals ignore cultural pressures for crime that emanate from the American Dream itself, from its celebration of the unrestrained, competitive pursuit of monetary success. Greater equality of opportunity and a redistribution of economic resources would not by themselves diminish the importance of winning and losing, nor would they eliminate the strong temptations to try to win by any means necessary.

Unintended Consequences of Liberal Reform Not only do liberal crime control strategies fail to target the full range of social causes of high crime rates in the United States, but, like conservative strategies, they are self-defeating when enacted in the absence of more fundamental social change. Policies that reduce discriminatory barriers to occupational achievement and broaden access to education, to the extent that they are successful, promote social mobility and extend the reach of the American Dream to persons and groups who have historically been excluded from its benefits. This is, of course, the very point of much liberal social policy. But, in so doing, these policies reinforce the commitment to the American Dream itself and hence sustain its criminogenic consequences. A population would not long remain wedded to the idea that everyone should struggle relentlessly to get ahead if hardly anyone actually ever did get ahead.[26]

In addition, the social mobility fostered by liberal social reform may aggravate the crime problem in another way, as suggested by the sociologist William Julius Wilson. Wilson describes the process through which poverty, crime, and other social problems become concentrated in urban neighborhoods. When better-off residents depart for other areas of the city or the suburbs, they take with them skills, resources, and models of conventional behavior that contribute to community stability. They leave behind, all else equal, a community that is less able to offer support for law-abiding behavior, less able to exercise informal social control over its members, less able to protect itself from outsiders, and therefore more vulnerable to crime. As crime rates rise, more residents depart, again those with the best prospects being the first to go. The concentration of economic and social disadvantage increases, and crime rates continue to climb.[27]

Wilson's analysis of neighborhood transition draws heavily on the social disorganization tradition associated with the Chicago School, which dominated urban sociology in the early part of the twentieth century; in fact, he illustrates his argument with data from Chicago community areas. Writing several decades later, however, Wilson supplements his analysis with an account of the growth in mobility opportunities for middle- and working-class blacks that accompanied declines in discriminatory barriers in education and work, and, to a more limited degree, housing during the 1960s and 1970s. The opening of the opportunity structure enabled many, though far from all, blacks to join the urban exodus of the previous 30 years. Even blacks who did not leave the central city because of continuing residential discrimination in suburban areas were able in greater numbers than ever before to move away from "declining" neighborhoods. As whites had been able to do for decades, blacks could now abandon old and deteriorating neighborhoods for new, more stable ones. They could participate in the American tradition of linking geographic and social mobility. Now, like other Americans, when they moved up, they could move out. As a result, unintentional to be sure, expansions in opportunities for some black Americans led to expansions in crime rates for others.

We do not mean to exaggerate either the effects on neighborhood crime rates of the out-migration of better-off residents or, for that matter, the number of black Americans who have benefited from equal opportunity policies. Nor do we condone in any way the racial discrimination that "kept blacks in their place" in earlier periods. Further, it would be absurd to blame those individuals, of whatever race, who flee crime-ridden communities in search of greater personal security. Their decisions and actions are understandable and, from the individual point of view, entirely justifiable.

We also do not mean to belittle the achievements of liberal social reform. The expansion of opportunities produces a broad range of benefits regardless of any impact on crime rates; there is more to improving the quality of life in a society than reducing the risks of criminal victimization. Providing everyone with the maximum feasible degree of opportunity for the realization of human potential is a worthy cultural goal as a matter of simple justice. Our point is simply that a war on poverty or on inequality of opportunity is not likely to be an effective strategy for crime control in the absence of other cultural and structural changes.

Beyond Liberalism and Conservatism

The failure of both liberals and conservatives to offer effective solutions to the crime problem ultimately reflects the inability, or unwillingness, of advocates of either approach to question the fundamental features of American society. In a sense, both are prisoners of the dominant culture. Conservatives and liberals alike embrace the American Dream without reservation and search for an external "enemy" with which to engage in a war. Conservatives direct the war against the "wicked" persons who are held to represent a danger to society.[28] The enemies for liberals are not bad persons but bad social conditions, imperfections of the social structure that make it difficult or impossible for some people to conform to dominant norms. These social imperfections, including poverty, racial discrimination, and lack of education, are typically viewed by liberals as a betrayal of the American Dream. Neither group entertains the possibility that the enemy comes from within, that the causes of crime lie within the dominant culture itself.

As a consequence of this intellectual blind spot, the policies of both conservatives and liberals are severely constrained by the logic of the existing culture and, in ironic ways, reflect this logic. The conservative approach promotes crime control policies without limits and at any cost. This expansive and expensive strategy for controlling crime embodies the anomic quality of American culture: the cultural imperative to pursue goals by any means necessary. Liberal policies, in contrast, strengthen the other element of American culture that is criminogenic—the excessive emphasis on the competitive, individualistic struggle for monetary success. Liberals propose, in effect, that strengthening the American Dream will solve the problems caused by the American Dream. In short, both liberal and conservative policies for crime control are ultimately self-defeating because they reproduce the very cultural and social conditions that generate the distinctively high levels of crime for which the United States is known throughout the world.

Any enduring reduction in crime will require moving beyond the flawed ideas and policies associated with both ends of the conventional political spectrum. However, the policies that we suggest are also not likely to bring about substantial reductions in crime in the short run. We are not aware of any policy solutions for the crime problem that could have this effect. The reason for this is not simply that past and present policies have been hamstrung by the liberal and conservative alternatives; it is also that the conditions that lead to crime cannot be ameliorated by "policy" as such, or at least by policy that is politically feasible. In the United States, substantial crime reductions require *social change,* not simply new social policy. Policy, on the other hand, is most often concerned with making existing arrangements more efficient. The function of policy is to improve existing means of achieving collective goals; rarely does policy seek to alter the goals themselves. As one analyst suggests, addressing the "basic causes" of a problem may be of little interest to policy makers because they are under strong political pressures to define problems in terms of available solutions, and they typically lack the material or political resources to alter basic causes.[29]

Genuine crime control requires transformation from within, reorganization of social institutions and regeneration of cultural commitments. This is certainly a formidable task given the powerful influence of existing cultural beliefs and the durability of structural arrangements. The task is not, however, an impossible one. Culture and social structure inevitably place constraints on human action, but these constraints are of a unique type. Unlike the limits imposed by the natural world, the social world is ultimately created and re-created by the participants themselves.

Sociologist Peter Berger uses the metaphor of a puppet show to describe the paradox of constraint and potentiality in human action.[30] He compares the expectations and requirements of social roles to the strings that regulate the movements of a puppet. The puppet's movements are, of course, constrained by the strings. At the same time, Berger cautions that the puppet metaphor should not be stretched too far. Human beings are not mindless puppets. Each of us individually can look up and examine the mechanism from which the strings hang, and, collectively, we can redesign the mechanism. Human actors, in other words, have the capacity to become aware of the social constraints on action and to change these constraints. In the next section, we sketch the kinds of changes in the institutional and cultural "mechanism" of American society that offer some promise of meaningful reductions in levels of serious crime.

CRIME REDUCTION THROUGH SOCIAL REORGANIZATION

Our prescriptions for crime reduction follow logically from our analysis of the causes of high levels of crime. To recapitulate very briefly: We contend that criminal activity is stimulated by strong cultural pressures for monetary success combined with anomie, a normative order with weak restraints on the selection of the means to pursue success. An institutional balance of power in which the economy assumes dominance over other social institutions accompanies this anomic cultural condition. Economic dominance diminishes the attractiveness of alternatives to the goal of monetary success and impedes the capacity of other institutions to perform their distinctive functions, including social control and social support. High levels of crime thus reflect intrinsic elements of American culture and the corrosive impact of these cultural elements on social structure.

It follows from this analysis, moving back up the causal chain from high levels of crime through social structure and culture, that crime reductions would result from policies that strengthen social structure and weaken the criminogenic qualities of American culture. More specifically, crime reductions would follow from policies and social changes that vitalize families, schools, and the political system, thereby enhancing the "drawing power" of the distinctive goals associated with these institutions and strengthening their capacity to exercise social control.[31] This institutional vitalization would, in turn, temper the anomic qualities and the intense pressures for monetary success associated with the American Dream. Finally, cultural regeneration—modifications in the American Dream itself—would promote and sustain institutional change and reduce cultural pressures for crime. We begin our discussion of social reorganization with a consideration of the structural dimension: institutional reform.

Institutional Reform

The Family and Schools Initiatives such as the provision of family leave, job sharing for husbands and wives, flexible work schedules, employer-provided child care, and a host of other "pro-family" economic policies should help alter the balance between the economic demands faced by parents and their obligations and opportunities to devote more time and energy to exclusively family concerns.[32] In many families, parents and children spend very little time with each other. In a survey in the early 1990s of American students in the sixth through the twelfth grades, half of the high school students reported that they did not share evening meals with their parents on a daily basis, and nearly half of the sixth graders reported that they spent two or more hours a day at home without an adult present.[33]

Policies that enable parents to spend more time with their children should not only strengthen family controls over children's behavior and enhance the social support available to children but also enable the schools to carry out their functions more effectively. Teachers and educational researchers alike maintain that the absence of parental support for education handicaps the schools in their efforts to motivate learning and keep children engaged in the educational process. Yet only about half of the ninth- and twelfth-graders in the previously cited survey above reported that their parents "talk with me about school." Only one-third reported that their parents attended school meetings or events.

These examples illustrate the point made in Chapter 4 concerning the interdependent nature of social institutions. The capacity of any institution to fulfill its distinctive function depends on the effective functioning of the others. Not surprisingly, then, the lack of articulation between the family and the schools has unfortunate consequences for society at large. As one educational researcher observes, the poor articulation between the home and the school reflects and reinforces a "serious erosion of social capital" in American communities. If children do not see adults often, and if their relationships with adults are "fleeting," adults cannot serve as effective deterrents and as positive influences on children's behavior. The social bonds necessary for discipline, emanating from both the family and the schools, weaken as a result.[34]

Policies aimed at strengthening the schools must proceed in concert with those designed to improve family functioning. These policies must confront two interrelated problems: (1) strengthening external controls and (2) strengthening the engagement of people—parents and teachers, as well as children and students—in the distinctive goals and "logics" of these institutions. It is worth pondering the mixed messages that our society currently sends regarding the best way to repair and strengthen families and schools.

The message regarding families is to avoid having one as long as possible. It is difficult to think of a single source of cultural encouragement in the United States today for young people to get married and to have children—in either order. In the current obsession with out-of-wedlock births, it is scarcely noticed that birthrates among young women have declined sharply since 1960. The proportion of births to unmarried women has risen, but this has happened because marriage rates have fallen even faster than birthrates. Over 85 percent of males and around 74 percent of females between the ages of 20 and 24 were single (that is, never married) in 2002, compared with 55 percent of males and 36 percent of females in this age group in 1970. Over the same period, the percentage of males in their late twenties who were single grew from 19 to 54 percent. Thirty-four percent of males in their early thirties were single in 2002, compared with less than 10 percent two decades earlier. Although in each age group females were more likely than males to be married, the fraction remaining single grew just as rapidly.[35]

The apparent decline in the attractiveness of marriage in the United States is a cause for some concern given the central role that marriage plays in creating what anthropologist David Murray refers to as "bridges of social connectedness." Marriages give rise to reciprocal obligations that bind not only the spouses themselves but also other family members and friends on both sides. This in turn promotes "moral feelings of attachment and integration" that help hold a society and culture together. In Murray's words, "Individual marriages are the rivets of the social order, local-level attachments by which the whole structure is ultimately assembled."[36]

Yet the loud message to young people is to stop having children rather than to start forming families. Whatever the salutary effects of this message, it serves to reinforce the view of families as burdens to be shouldered only after a long period of economic preparation. We do not necessarily advocate early marriage as a form of crime control, but it seems that a society with a professed commitment to "family values" should provide more cultural and social support for family formation. As a practical matter, this support will require lessening the dependence of marital and family decision making on purely economic considerations.

With respect to schools, a popular message sounds the market-oriented theme of "choice": Bad schools will be driven out of business by good ones if obstacles blocking open markets in schooling are eliminated. This will occur if people are given the options of purchasing their educations in either public or private schools and of enrolling in schools outside specific attendance areas or districts. Again, although such proposals may have particular merits, their general effect is to reinforce the market mentality of American education.[37] One can scarcely blame students for asking whether this or that aspect of their education "pays" when this is exactly the question that dominates current educational policy discussion.

A rather different type of policy for schools is suggested by our argument. Schools should be enabled to devote themselves to their distinctive goal of formal learning. This requires, as we have suggested, stronger parental support for the educational function. However, it also requires that children's economic prospects become tied less closely to their performance in school.

Those who look back fondly to the "good old days" of strict discipline and respect for learning that are supposed to have once characterized the American public school system often forget that one reason the schools could educate more effectively in the past is that they did not have to educate as universally. In a world where labor markets offered jobs that did not require a high school education, the public schools operated much more selectively than they do now. Students who flunked out or who were expelled for disciplinary reasons, or who left because they simply did not like school, did not as a rule end up in the streets; they went to work, they formed families, or they joined the military.

Not long ago, Americans depended less on schools for economic rewards. As recently as 1960, only 43 percent of whites and 20 percent of blacks aged 25 and older had completed four or more years of high school. By 2002, 85 percent of whites and 79 percent of blacks in this age group had completed high school.[38] In a society where "good jobs" require a college degree or some other form of training beyond high school, and where military service requires a high school diploma, schools will daily confront students who, at best, calculate their "investment" in education according to future earnings. At worst, they will find themselves in chronic conflicts with students made hopeless by the knowledge that proper educational certification is a necessary—but far from sufficient—condition for economic success.

We harbor no illusions that the manufacturing-based economy of the past, which provided well-paying jobs for those with minimal educational credentials, is likely to reappear. Nevertheless, skilled crafts continue to be important today, and many highly technical positions associated with the "information age" require training distinct from that generally provided in colleges and universities. While the conventional approach to market-oriented educational reform continues to pressure existing institutions of higher learning into "partnerships" designed to better serve the needs of the local business community, an alternative strategy would be to invest more heavily in parallel routes for occupational advancement that would better serve the needs of those who are primarily interested in "training" rather than "education" in the broad sense of the term.

The Polity   Turning to the institution of the polity, our analysis points to two types of policy shifts: (1) reform of the formal system of crime control, particularly sentencing policy and the correctional system, and (2) the creation of broader patterns of social participation, support, and control beyond the criminal justice system.

Corrections Policy   Corrections policy that is consistent with our analysis of the crime problem begins with a fundamental question that neither the liberal nor the conservative camp addresses: What is the optimum proportion of the population that should be under the jurisdiction of correctional agencies?[39] One may be tempted to answer zero to this question, but unless we are willing to assume a crime rate of zero or are willing to let all convicted offenders go unpunished, some proportion of the population must be under some form of correctional control at all times. So, again, what is the optimum proportion?

This is not a "policy question" narrowly defined; it is a question designed to stimulate a different way of thinking about crime control policy. It is a political question, and it most certainly is a moral question, because it requires judgments about the goals of crime control and not simply choices among more efficient or less efficient means to achieve a predefined goal, or, as in current policy, among several ill-defined and conflicting goals.[40]

A central goal of any approach to crime control that is based on our analysis is to reduce cultural support for crime. A prerequisite for accomplishing this objective is to end the war on crime. We are not proposing, of course, to end efforts at crime control. On the contrary, we believe that effective crime control can begin only when control is gained over current crime policy. Achieving control of crime policy requires placing limits on the costs of crime control, especially the costs of corrections. Although cost containment will not be easy, it is essential if the anomic and perverse consequences of the war on crime are to be halted.

The most effective way to achieve greater control over the explosive growth in incarceration—the most costly consequence of the war on crime—is through sentencing reform. The major impetus for escalating rates of imprisonment in the United States is not increasing rates of crime but sentencing policies such as mandatory-minimum sentences, so-called three-strikes statutes, truth-in-sentencing requirements, and related measures that have greatly increased both the proportion of convicted offenders serving prison sentences and the length of time they serve in prison.[41] These policies, along with greatly enhanced penalties for drug law violations, are the guts of the conservative agenda for crime control. Although they have resulted in some reduction in crime, that reduction has come at a cost, economic and social, that has begun to worry even many conservatives. For example, prominent conservative intellectual Glenn Loury maintains that "accumulating evidence demonstrates that the punitive anti-drug crusade of the last decade is, in fact, not producing benefits commensurate with its substantial costs."[42]

Control over the growth and costs of imprisonment can be achieved by sensible alterations in prison admission and release policies, alternative sentencing for drug offenders, sun-setting mandatory-minimum and truth-in-sentencing requirements, and placing more offenders under intensive supervision in the community. Capacity-sensitive admission and age-sensitive release policies appear especially promising.

Capacity-sensitive admission policies require judges to consider the availability of prison space as they decide whether convicted offenders are to serve their sentence in prison or on probation under supervision in the community. The availability of prison beds, in turn, is calculated according to budgetary restraints, existing prison capacity, and, ideally, legislative mandates or guidelines that establish a preset limit on the total number of prisoners. Capacity-sensitive policies have proven effective where they have been tried, notably in Minnesota (which had the second lowest state imprisonment rate, after Maine, as of mid-year 2003), in controlling prison population growth without diminishing public safety.[43] Capacity-sensitive policies would lead to larger numbers of offenders supervised in the community, but at greatly reduced costs per capita, even for those under intensive supervision.

Age-sensitive release policies take advantage of a well-known criminological fact: the decline in criminal offending with age. Offenders begin to terminate their "criminal careers" as they age, with an escalation in the termination rate after the early 40s.[44] It follows, from a public-safety perspective, that the use of scarce prison space becomes increasingly inefficient as offenders age, as it also becomes more costly, given the greater medical services required by older inmates. Where possible prison release policies, and where necessary sentencing policies, should give preference to older offenders (those beyond the age of 40), who should be supervised in the community unless they pose a demonstrable threat to public safety or have committed a serious violent crime.

Several states have begun to reform sentencing statutes and guidelines for drug offenders.[45] Persons convicted of drug possession rather than selling, who do not have a record of violence, should be supervised in the community and enrolled in mandatory treatment programs. The higher costs of community supervision and treatment would be more than offset by the reduction in the costs of imprisoning non-violent drug offenders.

Sunset provisions should be introduced into mandatory-minimum and truth-in-sentencing statutes.[46] Such policies have dubious benefits when crime rates are increasing; they have diminishing returns when crime rates are flat or falling. Legislatures would have much greater flexibility in the use of these policies, and would be more likely to demand evidence of their benefits, if they contained sunset provisions that require them to be periodically re-enacted.

In one way or another, each of the policy reforms we have recommended would increase the number of convicted offenders serving sentences under community supervision. The United States overutilizes the extremes of available punishment options (imprisonment and ordinary probation) and underutilizes probation under intensive supervision. Only about one in five persons serving criminal sentences in the community are under so-called intensive supervision. The great majority is minimally and haphazardly supervised, largely due to the huge caseloads, averaging over 70 per supervisor, carried by community corrections officials. As two criminal justice experts have noted, "The current community corrections system largely reproduces the behavior of the rest of the criminal justice system: It makes many demands, spottily monitors compliance, and punishes detected deviations slowly and unpredictably, but often quite severely."[47] Placing more persons under intensive supervision involving frequent contact with probation or parole officers, employment or training requirements, drug testing, drug treatment, curfews, electronic monitoring, and family and other social supports—and swift and certain sanctions for failure to comply with supervision requirements—would raise the cost of community corrections. But it would lower the cost of imprisonment and holds out the promise of behavioral change, something prisons in the United States no longer even promise, much less deliver.

Something akin to a social movement, involving community activists, social service and treatment providers, academics, and ex-prisoners, has emerged recently under the banner of *prisoner reentry*.[48] The reentry movement has stimulated new thinking and programs dealing with the transition from prison back to the community. Some models of prisoner reentry would have the sentencing court oversee the reentry process; others place the responsibility for reentry with community corrections in partnership with social service and law enforcement agencies. No matter the design, the basic idea is to build a bridge between prison and community for returning prisoners. In the ideal case, returning prisoners would receive assistance in securing suitable housing, accessing training and employment, reuniting with families, and meeting physical and mental health needs. Along with social support, the reentry process should entail a system of graduated sanctions for failure to comply with the conditions of community supervision, including counseling, residential treatment, increased supervision level, electronic monitoring, curfew, loss of travel privileges, increased drug testing, and confinement to a halfway house. Reincarceration would be used only as a last resort for those offenders who continue to violate supervision rules or who commit new crimes. The promise of such programs is that, by offering real incentives for conformity and maintenance of a crime-free lifestyle, the growth in the prison population can be controlled without jeopardizing public safety.

Despite the popularity of prisoner reentry programs—President Bush promoted them in his 2004 State of the Union Address—in most states they remain in the formative stage. Although advocates claim they will save money by reducing returns to prison for so-called technical violations of the conditions of community supervision and protect communities by providing incentives for lawful behavior, evidence of such benefits has not yet been produced. Nonetheless, in our view, they hold great advantages over present policy. They are premised on the necessity to imprison people who commit serious crimes *and* the necessity to reintegrate them upon their release—a philosophy of "locking 'em up" without throwing away the key.[49] They offer hope and support to released prisoners, but they also require responsible behavior in return, not only from released prisoners but also from public officials.

Reconciling tough choices over cost, safety, and justice presupposes some agreement over the priorities of what is still quaintly called "corrections" policy. Current policy is politically pleasing because it allows policy makers to behave irresponsibly. It does not require consensus building or difficult trade-offs among competing values and interests. It does not require appreciation of the consequences, budgetary or human, of policy choices, beyond the symbolic benefit of acting tough on crime. The approach we prefer–reigning in sentencing laws and planning for the transition from prison back to the community—does not have this spurious benefit because, by introducing a measure of restraint into crime control policy, it would end the costly anything-goes punishment spree that has vastly expanded formal social control without a commensurate reduction in crime.

National Service   Reforms that are limited to the criminal justice system, however, will not by themselves produce appreciable reductions in crime. Broader changes within the polity are necessary to nurture the sense of collective obligation and individual duty essential for the effective functioning of formal social controls. One proposal that appears especially promising in this respect is the creation of a national service corps. If it is to contribute to crime control, such a system must be universalistic and involve an array of opportunities and obligations to serve local communities and the society as a whole. It can perform a particularly important integrative function by providing education, training in needed skills, and meaningful social controls for adolescents and young adults who have graduated from or dropped out of traditional schools and have not availed themselves of the kinds of alternative educational routes previously referred to, have not found work that will lead to a career, and who have outgrown the reach of their parents but have not yet formed families of their own. In short, by offering an institutional mooring for young people during the transition to adulthood, national service promises to bolster social control and facilitate "maturational reform," that is, the process through which young people involved in common forms of delinquency turn away from illegal behavior as they mature and assume adult obligations.

A specific form of national service with direct relevance to crime control policy is a Police Corps of young people trained as police officers who would serve on local forces for periods of two to four years. President Bill Clinton endorsed the concept in the early 1990s as part of his proposal to provide college assistance in return for community service. One commentator advocated the Police Corps as the basis for President Clinton's efforts to build support for his broader philosophy of national service: "It's the logical place to start now, as the new President embarks on his most ambitious goal—to rebuild a national sense of community, responsibility, and public altruism."[50]

Although the Police Corps was not implemented, President Clinton was able to establish the Corporation for National and Community Service, better known as AmeriCorps. AmeriCorps is a voluntary program of community service with strong crime prevention and public safety objectives. The program is open to persons of all ages; however, most volunteers are young adults who receive a living allowance and money toward college in return for their one or two years of service. After succeeding the Clinton administration, President Bush embraced the concept of AmeriCorps and asked for an expansion of its work to assist in homeland security. Given its modest size (it was funded at $425 million in 2002) and voluntary nature, AmeriCorps does not significantly alter the level or quality of social participation by young people in the United States. Nevertheless, it serves as a prototype for the kind of political reform that, by actively engaging the young in community service, strengthens the sense of collective goal attainment that is the central and distinguishing function of the polity.[51]

Social Stratification and the Economy   Finally, our analysis has important implications for the system of social stratification and the interrelations between this system and the economy. The relationship between stratification and crime has been the focus of extensive research and theorizing in modern criminology. Conventional approaches to the stratification-crime relationship, however, direct attention almost exclusively to a single feature of the stratification system: the distribution of opportunities for economic rewards. These explanations typically attribute crime to inequality in economic opportunities. We have maintained that greater equality of opportunity is not likely to eliminate pressures to succeed at any cost. The mere existence of unequal outcomes is likely to generate such pressures, regardless of the openness of the stratification system, if monetary success reigns supreme as a cultural goal and the economy dominates the institutional structure of society.

It might seem on the surface that the solution to the crime problem lies in greater equality of outcomes. However, it is not merely the shape of the distribution of material and symbolic rewards in America that contributes to crime but rather the mechanism by which rewards are distributed. In this respect, our analysis is informed by Marx's insight that the distribution of the means of consumption is ultimately dependent on the "conditions of production themselves."[52] The conditions of production in American society dictate that the distribution of rewards be tied to economic functions: either the performance of occupational roles or the possession of capital. In other words, the wealth that is produced within the economy is also distributed almost exclusively in accordance with economic criteria by labor and capital markets. To shore up such other institutions as the family, schools, and the polity relative to the economy, a greater share of the national wealth will have to be allocated on the basis of noneconomic criteria.

We are not endorsing the nationalization of the means of production to rebalance institutions. The political and economic failures of state socialist societies have been made glaringly apparent by the course of history. Rather, the model of the mixed economies in Europe and Japan appears promising. These nations have implemented a wide range of social policies and programs to ensure that material well-being is not strictly tied to economic functions and to guarantee that noneconomic roles receive meaningful financial support from collective resources.

Evidence suggests, moreover, that governmental efforts to "tame the market" by providing guarantees of minimal levels of material well-being are associated with comparatively low levels of serious crime. Figure 5.1 depicts the relationship between the average homicide rate over the 1980–1990 period and a measure of the extensiveness and generosity of social welfare policies for a sample of 18 advanced capitalist nations. The political scientist Gosta Esping-Andersen created the welfare measure, referred to as the "decommodification index." The index reflects the ease of access to welfare entitlements, their income replacement value, and the range of social statuses and conditions that they cover. High scores on this index indicate comprehensive and unrestrictive welfare policies, whereas low scores indicate welfare systems characterized by relatively low benefit levels and strict eligibility requirements.

The relationship revealed in Figure 5.1, although not a perfectly linear one, is consistent with our theoretical explanation of societal levels of crime.[53] Capitalist nations that limit dependence on the market for material well-being, as reflected in high decommodification scores, tend to exhibit comparatively low homicide rates. In contrast, nations in which citizens are highly dependent on market outcomes for their basic survival tend to have comparatively high homicide rates, with the United States serving as a striking case in point. The mechanism through which material rewards are distributed in capitalist societies—specifically, the extent to which market forces are moderated and counterbalanced by the welfare state—thus appears to be related to overall levels of the most serious of crimes, criminal homicide.[54]

In summary, the structural changes that could lead to significant reductions in crime are those that promote a rebalancing of social institutions. These changes would involve reducing the subordination to the economy of the family, schools, the polity, and the general system of social stratification. Most of the specific proposals for institutional change that we have put forth are not particularly novel. They have been advanced by others in different contexts and with different agendas. These proposals, however, typically are considered in isolation from one another. For example, conservatives who bemoan the demise of the family and call for its rejuvenation rarely pursue the logical implications of their analyses and proposals. They fail to recognize or acknowledge that the vitalization

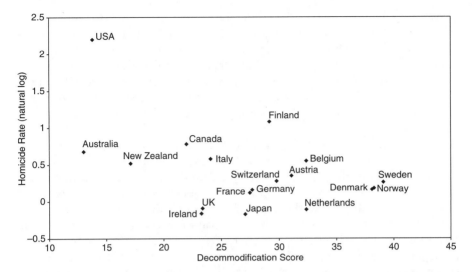

FIGURE 5.1 Scatterplot of Homicide Rates and Decommodification Scores for 18 Advanced Nations

of the family requires changes in the economy that are likely to be very distasteful to conservatives on ideological grounds.

The distinctive and powerful feature of the sociological paradigm is that it directs attention to the interconnections among social institutions. Because of these interconnections, piecemeal reforms are likely to be ineffective. Moreover, our analytical framework implies that institutional reforms must go hand in hand with cultural change because culture and institutional structures are themselves inextricably bound. It is to the matter of cultural change that we now turn.

THE TASK OF CULTURAL REGENERATION

A basic premise of this book is that the beliefs, values, and goals associated with the American Dream are firmly entrenched in the American historical experience and consciousness. If this premise is correct, it would be fanciful to entertain the possibility of any wholesale rejection of the American Dream.[55] Such a radical cultural transformation is not required, however, to begin the process of enriching noneconomic institutions. Instead, by moderating the excesses of the dominant cultural ethos and emphasizing its useful features, institutional reform can be stimulated, and significant reductions in crime can be realized.

We have characterized the American Dream as the commitment to the goal of monetary success, to be pursued by all members of society, under conditions of open, individual competition. The most important and valuable theme running through this cultural ethos is that of a universal entitlement to strive for a better life, which can be attained as a consequence of one's own achievements. In other words, the American Dream empowers everyone to dream about a brighter future and participate in the creation of that future. This vision of possibilities, of hope, is liberating, and it serves the interests of both individuals and the larger society by inspiring people to develop their talents and abilities.

The criminogenic tendencies of the American Dream derive from its *exaggerated* emphasis on monetary success and its resistance to limits on the means for the pursuit of success. Any significant lessening of the criminogenic consequences of the dominant culture thus requires the taming of its strong materialistic pressures and the creation of a greater receptivity to socially imposed restraints. To dampen the materialistic pressures, goals other than the accumulation of wealth will have to be elevated to a position of prominence in the cultural hierarchy. This implies greater recognition of and appreciation for the institutional realms that are currently subservient to the economy. More specifically, social roles such as parenting, "partnering," teaching, learning, and serving the community will have to become, as ends in themselves, meaningful alternatives to material acquisition. Furthermore, enhancing the respect for these noneconomic roles implies that money will no longer serve as the principal gauge of social achievement and personal worth. Money will not be, in the words of Marian Wright Edelman, the preeminent "measure of our success."[56]

The other, complementary, task of cultural regeneration will involve fostering a cultural receptivity to restraints. The dominant cultural ethos glorifies the individual pursuit of material well-being. People are encouraged to maximize personal utility, to be guided by self-interest, and to regard others as potential competitors in the race for economic rewards. However, many of the institutional reforms to which we point entail the subordination of individual interests to larger collectivities, such as the family, neighbors, and the community. It seems unlikely that social change conducive to lower levels of crime will occur in the absence of a cultural reorientation that encompasses an enhanced emphasis on the importance of mutual support and collective obligations and a decreased emphasis on individual rights, interests, and privileges.[57] In short, a reoriented and tempered American Dream would reflect the realization that "in dreams begin responsibilities."

AN INTELLECTUAL FOUNDATION FOR CHANGE

An important intellectual component accompanies the task of balancing social obligations with individual interests. The extreme individualism of American culture impedes a full understanding of the interdependencies between the individual and society. Human beings are inherently social beings. As a consequence, their individual development and maturation presuppose social relationships that are necessarily constraining. To borrow from Marx once again, "Only in association with others has each individual the means of cultivating his [or her] talents in all directions."[58]

The idea that individual growth requires social motivation, support, and regulation forms part of the distinctive corpus of classical sociological thought. It figures significantly not only in Marx's analysis of capitalist society but also in George Herbert Mead's theory of the social formation of the self and in Émile Durkheim's conception of the collective conscience.[59] It is one of the few ideas in the history of sociological thought that is not readily identified as belonging to one or another intellectual or ideological camp. It links the micro- and the macrolevels of analysis and informs conflict theories of social change as well as consensus theories of social order. As a defining element in the common heritage of the discipline, it prepares the conceptual ground for a sociological reappraisal of the American Dream.

This reappraisal suggests that different parts of the American Dream work at cross-purposes. Its universalism and achievement orientation inspire ambition and in so doing stimulate the motivational dynamic necessary for the realization of human potential. However, its exaggerated materialism and extreme individualism narrow the range of human capacities that receive cultural respect and social support and discourage people from assuming obligations that in principle could be liberating. By clarifying this internal contradiction, a sociological understanding of the American Dream can help lay the intellectual groundwork for the cultural and institutional changes necessary for reducing crime in our society.

TOWARD A MATURE SOCIETY

In closing, we return to James Truslow Adams for a final observation on the legacy and the future of the American Dream. Adams traces the possibilities of the Dream to the American Revolution. The cultural significance of the revolt lay in "the breaking down of all spiritual barriers to the complete development of whatever might prove to be fertile, true, and lasting in the American dream."[60] However, Adams laments the fact that this developmental potential was inhibited by the "debilitating doctrine" that, two centuries after its birth, the United States is still a "young" nation. He asks

> Is it not time to proclaim that we are not children but men
> [and women] who must put away childish things; that we have
> overlooked that fact too long; that we have busied ourselves
> overmuch with fixing up the new place we moved into 300 years
> ago, with making money in the new neighborhood; and that we
> should begin to live a sane, maturely civilized life?[61]

The promise of a mature America is the cultural encouragement for all persons to develop their full range of talents and capacities on the basis of mutual support and collective obligations. Adams's American Dream, and ours, must be reinvented so that its destructive consequences can be curbed, and so that its fertile, true, and lasting promise of human betterment can be fulfilled.

NOTES

1. Edelman (1992, p. 89).
2. "In Dreams Begin Responsibilities" is the title of Delmore Schwartz's short story originally published in *Partisan Review* in 1937. It is reprinted in Schwartz ([1937] 1978, pp. 1–9).
3. Adams ([1929] 1969, p. 143).
4. Ibid., p. 122.
5. Ibid., p. 123.
6. Ibid., pp. 101, 116.
7. Ibid., p. 142.
8. Ibid., p. 143.
9. Blumstein (1993, p. 10). The NCRP data on prison admissions are reported in BJS (1992, p. 8).
10. Spelman (2000).
11. The data for 2002 are from the Bureau of Justice Statistics (BJS) reported in Harrison and Karberg (2003). The 1985 figures are from Gilliard and Beck (1997). Good discussions of the increase in levels of incarceration of the 1980s and 1990s can be found in Blumstein and Beck (1999) and Mauer (1999).
12. The corrections expenditure data are from the Bureau of Justice Statistics (www.ojp.usdoj/bjs), accessed August 19, 2004.
13. The percentage growth in correctional populations between 1985 and 2002 was computed from BJS data (http://www.ojp.usdoj.gov/bjs), accessed August 20, 2004.
14. Blumstein (1993, p. 5). For a penetrating and disturbing discussion of the disparate impact of the drug war on African-Americans, see Tonry (1995).
15. See Steinberg (1981, pp. 194–200) for a discussion of the role of the Black Codes in the "reconstruction of black servitude" after the Civil War.
16. See Spelman (2000) for an appraisal of the evidence linking the expansion in incarceration to changes in crime rates.
17. See Walker (1989, pp. 153–159) for a review of arguments surrounding plea bargaining as an adaptation to large caseloads and for a discussion of realistic reforms of this widespread practice.
18. Feeley and Simon (1992).
19. For research on the relationship between sex ratios and family relations, see Messner and Sampson (1991) and South and Trent (1988). See also Sampson (1987) for evidence concerning the effects of family disruption on rates of black violence, and Rose and Clear (1998) on the impact of incarceration on community social organization.
20. Quoted in Blumstein (1993, p. 11).

21. Cloward and Ohlin (1960).

22. See Liska and Messner (1999, pp. 49–50) for a description of the Mobilization for Youth program and a discussion of research assessing its effectiveness.

23. Sidel (1986, p. 110).

24. See Wilson (1975, chap. 1).

25. Routine activities theory, which links crime to variations in the behavior of victims rather than to the motivations of offenders, was introduced as a distinctive approach in criminology by Cohen and Felson (1979). For a general discussion of this approach, see Felson (1998).

26. This point is elaborated in Rosenfeld (1989, pp. 459–462).

27. See Wilson (1987, especially chap. 2; 1996).

28. Wilson (1975, p. 235).

29. Gilsinan (1990, pp. 5–6). For a historical perspective on the limits of the criminal justice system as a means of crime control, see Friedman (1993).

30. Berger (1963, p. 121).

31. The sociologist Gary LaFree (1998) similarly emphasizes the importance of institutional revitalization for significant reductions in crime in the U.S.

32. A modest step toward such policies was taken by President Clinton in 2000 when he issued an executive order banning employment discrimination against parents. The order did not require congressional approval and applies only to federal workers (*St. Louis Post-Dispatch*, 2000).

33. Mansnerus (1993). See also Presser (2003). Levitan, Belous, and Gallo (1988) provide an excellent overview of the relationship between the family and other institutions, and numerous proposals for strengthening family functioning.

34. Interview with Randall Curran reported in Mansnerus (1993, p. 14).

35. The data for 1970 are from U.S. Bureau of the Census (1998). The data for 2002 were retrieved online at http://www.census.gov/prod/www/statistical-abstract-03.html.

36. Murray (1994). The quotations are from pages 9, 14, and 15.

37. For an extended discussion and critique of proposals to reform the public schools through the introduction of market mechanisms, see Henig (1994). Henig argues that advocates of market reform tend to ignore the collective purposes of education, and their market-based proposals often threaten to "erode the public forums in which decisions with societal consequences can democratically be resolved" (p. 200).

38. The data on educational attainment come from the U.S. Bureau of the Census (http://www.census.gov/prod/www/statistical-abstract-03.html).

39. The approach to correctional policy introduced in this section is discussed more fully in Rosenfeld and Kempf (1991).

40. On the conflicting goals of correctional policy, see Thomas (1987).

41. See Blumstein and Beck (1999).

42. Quoted in Teles and Kleiman (2000, p. 30).

43. Blumstein (2002, pp. 478-480). Mid-year 2003 state incarceration rates are reported in Harrison and Karberg (2003).

44. On the relationship between age and crime, see Gottfredson and Hirschi (1990). See Blumstein (2002, p. 477) for a discussion of the termination of criminal careers.

45. *USA Today* (2002). See the website for the Campaign for New Drug Policies (www.drugreform.org) for a comprehensive description of reform efforts around the country.

46. Truth-in-sentencing laws require convicted offenders to serve a minimum proportion (typically 85%) of their sentence in prison. See Ditton and Wilson (1999).

47. Teles and Kleiman (2000). For data on probation and parole supervision levels, caseloads, and costs, see Camp and Camp (2002).

48. See Petersilia (1999); Travis (2001); Travis, Solomon, and Waul (2001).

49. Zimring (2001, p. 146) describes the "new politics of punishment" in the U.S. as a shift in emphasis from 'lock 'em up' to 'lock 'em up and throw away the key.'

50. Klein (1992).

51. Information about AmeriCorps is available at http://www.americorps.org.

52. See the "Critique of the Gotha Programme" in Marx and Engels (1968, pp. 315–335; quoted material is from p. 325).

53. Esping-Andersen (1990) reports decommodification scores in his incisive analysis of different welfare state regimes, *The Three Worlds of Welfare Capitalism*. Following conventional practice for dealing with highly skewed dependent variables in linear modeling, the homicide rates in Figure 5.1 are expressed in terms of natural logarithms. We also find an inverse relationship between decommodification and homicide rates in a multivariate analysis based on a larger sample of nations ($N = 45$). This analysis includes statistical controls for a wide range of demographic and socioeconomic characteristics of nations. See Messner and Rosenfeld (1997).

54. For thoughtful discussions of potential dangers for the balance among social institutions of expanding the welfare state, see Habermas (1989) and Wolfe (1989). A more extensive discussion of the results of quantitative assessments of our basic theoretical argument can be found in Messner (2004).

55. See Hochschild (1995, pp. 258–260) for a similar appraisal.

56. *The Measure of Our Success* is the title of Edelman's (1992) book from which her quotation at the beginning of this chapter is taken.

57. See Braithwaite (1989, pp. 168–174).

58. Quoted in Bottomore and Rubel (1964, p. 247). For a more contemporary reaffirmation of this basic sociological premise, see Bellah et al. (1991, p. 6).

59. Berger and Luckmann (1966) provide an excellent treatment of the "dialectic" between the individual and society.

60. Quoted in Nevins (1968, p. 70).

61. Adams ([1929] 1969, p. 256).

References

ABCNEWS.com. 2004. "Conviction Clouds Martha Stewart's Future" (March 9). www.abcnews.com.

Adams, James Truslow. 1931. *The Epic of America*. Boston: Little, Brown.

———. [1929] 1969. *Our Business Civilization: Some Aspects of American Culture*. New York: AMS Press.

Adler, Freda. 1983. *Nations Not Obsessed with Crime*. Littleton, CO.: Rothman.

Adler, Freda, and William S. Laufer. 1995. *The Legacy of Anomie Theory*. New Brunswick, NJ: Transaction.

Adler, William M. 1995. *Land of Opportunity: One Family's Quest for the American Dream in the Age of Crack*. New York: Atlantic Monthly Press.

Agnew, Robert. 1992. "Foundation for a General Strain Theory of Crime and Delinquency." *Criminology* 30:47–87.

Akers, Ronald L., Marvin D. Krohn, Lonn Lanza-Kaduce, and Marcia Radosevich. 1979. "Social Learning and Deviant Behavior." *American Sociological Review* 44:636–655.

Alba, Richard D., and Steven F. Messner. 1995. "*Point Blank* Against Itself: Evidence and Inference About Guns, Crime, and Gun Control." *Journal of Quantitative Criminology* 11:391–410.

Albany Times-Union. 1995. "Gingrich Promotes His Reading Program." March 2, p. A6.

Alter, Jonathan. 1992. "The Body Count at Home." *Newsweek*, December 28, p. 55.

———. 1993. "There's a War On at Home." *Newsweek*, September 27, p. 42.

Anderson, Elijah. 1999. *Code of the Street: Decency, Violence, and the Moral Life of the Inner City*. New York: W. W. Norton.

Anderson, Robert N., and Betty L. Smith. 2003. "Deaths: Leading Causes for 2001." *National Vital Statistics Reports*. 52: 9 (November 7).

Archer, Dane, and Rosemary Gartner. 1984. *Violence and Crime in Cross-National Perspective*. New Haven, CT: Yale University Press.

Babbie, Earl. 1992. *The Practice of Social Research*. 6th ed. Belmont, CA: Wadsworth.

Bailey, Kenneth D. 1987. *Methods of Social Research*. 3d ed. New York: Free Press.

Barclay, Gordon, and Cynthia Tavares. 2002. *International Comparisons of Criminal Justice Statistics 2000*. London: Home Office. www.homeoffice.gov.uk.

Barstow, David. 2003a. "A Trench Caves In; a Young Worker is Dead. Is It a Crime?" *New York Times* (December 21). www.nytimes.com.

———. 2003b. "U.S. Rarely Seeks Charges for Deaths in Workplace." *New York Times* (December 22). www.nytimes.com.

Barstow, David, and Lowell Bergman. 2003. "Deaths on the Job, Slaps on the Wrist." *New York Times* (January 10). www.nytimes.com.

Bassis, Michael S., Richard J. Gelles, and Ann Levine. 1991. *Sociology: An Introduction*. 4th ed. New York: McGraw-Hill.

Baumer, Eric, Janet L. Lauritsen, Richard Rosenfeld, and Richard Wright. 1998. "The Influence of Crack Cocaine on Robbery, Burglary, and Homicide Rates: A Cross-City, Longitudinal Analysis." *Journal of Research in Crime and Delinquency* 35:316–340.

Bayley, David H. 1991. *Forces of Order: Policing Modern Japan*. Berkeley: University of California Press.

Beck, Melinda. 1993. "Mary Poppins Speaks Out." *Newsweek* (February 22), pp. 66–68.

Beeghley, Leonard. 2003. *Homicide: A Sociological Explanation*. Lanham, MD: Rowman & Littlefield.

Bellah, Robert N., Richard Madsen, William M. Sullivan, Ann Swidler, and Steven M. Tipton. 1985. *Habits of the Heart: Individualism and Commitment in American Life*. Berkeley: University of California Press.

———. 1991. *The Good Society*. New York: Knopf.

Berger, Peter L. 1963. *Invitation to Sociology: A Humanistic Perspective*. Garden City, NY: Anchor.

Berger, Peter L., and Thomas Luckmann. 1966. *The Social Construction of Reality: A Treatise in the Sociology of Knowledge*. Garden City, NY: Anchor.

Bernard, Thomas J. 1984. "Control Criticisms of Strain Theories: An Assessment of Theoretical and Empirical Adequacy." *Journal of Research in Crime and Delinquency* 21:353–372.

———. 1995. "Merton versus Hirschi: Who Is Faithful to Durkheim's Heritage?" Pages 81–90 in *The Legacy of Anomie Theory*, edited by Freda Adler and William S. Laufer. New Brunswick, NJ: Transaction.

Beutel, Ann M., and Margaret Mooney Marini. 1995. "Gender and Values." *American Sociological Review* 60:436–448.

Black, Donald. 1984. "Crime as Social Control." Pages 1–27 in *Toward a General Theory of Social Control*, vol. 2, edited by Donald Black. New York: Academic Press.

Blau, Peter M., and Judith R. Blau. 1982. "The Cost of Inequality: Metropolitan Structure and Violent Crime." *American Sociological Review* 47:114–129.

Block, Richard. 1998. *Firearms in Canada and Eight Other Western Countries: Selected Findings of the 1996 International Crime (Victim) Survey*. Working Document. Canadian Firearms Centre. Department of Justice, Canada.

Blumstein, Alfred. 1993. "Making Rationality Relevant—The American Society of Criminology 1992 Presidential Address." *Criminology* 31:1–16.

———. 1995. "Youth Violence, Guns and the Illicit-Drug Industry." *Journal of Criminal Law and Criminology* 86:10–36.

———. 2002. "Prisons: A Policy Challenge." Pp. 451–482 in *Crime: Public Policies for Crime Control*, edited by J. Q. Wilson and J. Petersilia. Oakland, CA: ICS Press.

Blumstein, Alfred, and Allen J. Beck. 1999. "Population Growth in U.S. Prisons, 1980–1996." Pp. 17–61 in *Crime and Justice*, vol. 86 (Prisons), edited by Michael Tonry and Joan Petersilia. Chicago: University of Chicago Press.

Blumstein, Alfred, and Richard Rosenfeld. 1998. "Explaining Recent Trends in U.S. Homicide Rates." *Journal of Criminal Law and Criminology* 88:1175–1216.

———. 1999. "Trends in Rates of Violence in the USA." *Studies on Crime and Crime Prevention* 8:139–167.

Blumstein, Alfred, and Joel Wallman, eds. 2000. *The Crime Drop in America*. New York: Cambridge University Press.

Bohlen, Celestine. 1996. "Where Everyday Is Mother's Day." *New York Times* (May 12), sec. 4, pp. 1–5.

Bottomore, T. B., and Maximilien Rubel. 1964. *Karl Marx: Selected Writings in Sociology and Social Philosophy*. New York: McGraw-Hill.

Braithwaite, John. 1989. *Crime, Shame and Reintegration*. New York: Cambridge University Press.

Bryan, Bill. 1992. "Neighborhood Crime Takes Deadly Toll: Elderly Man Dies after Robbery." *St. Louis Post-Dispatch* (August 25), p. 3A.

———. 1996. "Shooting Victim Was Help to Many." *St. Louis Post-Dispatch* (February 27), pp. 1A, 5A.

Bryan, Bill, and Joan Little. 1993. "Student, 17, Fatally Shot at Sumner." *St. Louis Post-Dispatch* (March 26), pp. 1A, 10A.

Bureau of Justice Statistics. 1992a. *Criminal Victimization in the United States, 1991*. Washington, DC: U.S. Department of Justice.

———. 1992b. *Prisoners in 1991*. Washington, DC: U.S. Department of Justice.

———. 1995a. *Correctional Populations in the United States*. Washington, DC: U.S. Department of Justice.

———. 1995b. *Prisoners in 1994*. Washington, DC: U.S. Department of Justice.

———. 1998. *Prisoners in 1997*. Washington, DC: U.S. Department of Justice.

———. 1999. *Correctional Populations in the United States, 1996*. Washington, DC: U.S. Department of Justice.

Burgess, Robert L., and Ronald L. Akers. 1966. "A Differential Association-Reinforcement Theory of Criminal Behavior." *Social Problems* 14:128–147.

Bursik, Robert J. Jr., 1988. "Social Disorganization and Theories of Crime and Delinquency: Problems and Prospects." *Criminology* 26:519–551.

Bursik, Robert J., Jr., and Harold Grasmick. 1993. *Neighborhoods and Crime: The Dimensions of Effective Community Control*. New York: Lexington Books.

Camp, Camile Graham, and George M. Camp. 2002. *The 2001 Corrections Yearbook: Adult Systems*. Middletown, CT: Criminal Justice Institute.

Caruso, David B. 2004. "Student Killings Prompt Protests in Philly." *Associated Press* (March 26). http://news.yahoo.com.

Celis III, William. 1993. "Corporate Rescuer Is Selected to Head Schools in California." *New York Times* (November 11), pp. A1, A12.

Chambliss, William J., and Robert B. Seidman. 1971. *Law, Order, and Power*. Reading, MA: Addison-Wesley.

Chapman, Stephen. 1992. "LA Jurors Blinded by Fear of Crime." *St. Louis Post-Dispatch* (May 4), p. 3B.

Cherlin, Andrew J. 1992. *Marriage, Divorce, Remarriage*. Revised and enlarged ed. Cambridge, MA: Harvard University Press.

Clinard, Marshall B., ed. 1964. *Anomie and Deviant Behavior: A Discussion and Critique*. New York: Free Press.

Clinard, Marshall B., and Peter C. Yeager. 1980. *Corporate Crime*. New York: Free Press.

Clines, Francis X. 1993. "An Unfettered Milken Has Lessons to Teach." *New York Times* (October 16), pp. 1, 9.

Cloward, Richard, and Lloyd E. Ohlin. 1960. *Delinquency and Opportunity: A Theory of Delinquent Gangs*. New York: Free Press.

Cohen, Albert K. 1955. *Delinquent Boys: The Culture of the Gang*. Glencoe, IL: Free Press.

———. 1985. "The Assumption That Crime Is a Product of Environments: Sociological Approaches." Pp. 223–243 in *Theoretical Methods in Criminology*, edited by Robert F. Meier. Beverly Hills, CA: Sage.

Cohen, Deborah Vidaver. 1995. "Ethics and Crime in Business Firms: Organizational Culture and the Impact of Anomie." Pp.183–206 in *The Legacy of Anomie Theory*, edited by Freda Adler and William S. Laufer. New Brunswick, NJ: Transaction.

Cohen, Lawrence E., and Marcus Felson. 1979. "Social Change and Crime Rate Trends: A Routine Activities Approach." *American Sociological Review* 44:588–608.

Cole, Stephen. 1975. "The Growth of Scientific Knowledge: Theories of Deviance as a Case Study." Pp. 175–220 in *The Idea of Social Structure: Papers in Honor of Robert K. Merton*, edited by Lewis A. Coser. New York: Harcourt Brace Jovanovich.

Coleman, James William. 1994. *The Criminal Elite: The Sociology of White Collar Crime*. 3d ed. New York: St. Martin's Press.

Coleman, Richard P., and Lee Rainwater. 1978. *Social Standing in America: New Dimensions of Class*. New York: Basic Books.

Columbia Encyclopedia. 1993 (http://www.infoplease.com/ce5/CE034431.html).

Colvin, Mark, and John Pauly. 1983. "A Critique of Criminology: Toward an Integrated Structural-Marxist Theory of Delinquency Production." *American Journal of Sociology* 89:513–551.

Conklin, John E. 2003. *Why Crime Rates Fell*. Boston, MA: Allyn and Bacon.

Cook, Philip J., and Mark H. Moore. 1999. "Guns, Gun Control, and Homicide: A Review of Research and Public Policy." Pp. 277–296 in *Homicide: A Sourcebook of Social Research*, edited by M. Dwayne Smith and Margaret A. Zahn. Thousand Oaks, CA: Sage.

Cook, Philip J., Mark H. Moore, and Anthony A. Braga. 2002. "Gun Control." Pp. 291–329 in *Crime: Public Policies for Crime Control*, edited by James Q. Wilson and Joan Petersilia. Oakland, CA: ICS Press.

Cork, Daniel. 1999. "Examining Space-Time Interaction in City-Level Homicide Data: Crack Markets and the Diffusion of Guns Among Youth." *Journal of Quantitative Criminology* 15:379–406.

Cullen, Francis T. 1983. *Rethinking Crime and Deviance Theory: The Emergence of a Structuring Tradition*. Totowa, NJ: Rowman & Allanheld.

———. 1988. "Were Cloward and Ohlin Strain Theorists? Delinquency and Opportunity Revisited." *Journal of Research in Crime and Delinquency* 25:214–241.

Cullen, Francis T., and John Paul Wright. 1997. "Liberating the Anomie-Strain Paradigm: Implications from Social-Support Theory." Pp. 187–206 in *The Future of Anomie Theory*, edited by Nikos Passas and Robert Agnew. Boston: Northeastern University Press.

Currie, Elliott. 1991. "Crime in the Market Society: From Bad to Worse in the Nineties." *Dissent* (Spring), pp. 254–259.

———. 1999. "Reflections on Crime and Criminology at the Millennium." *Western Criminology Review* 2(1). Online at http://wcr.sonoma.edu/v2n1/currie.html.

Curtis, Lynn A. 1975. *Violence, Race, and Culture*. Lexington, MA: Heath.

Derber, Charles. 1992. *Money, Murder and the American Dream: Wilding from Main Street to Wall Street*. Boston: Faber & Faber.

———. 1996. *The Wilding of America: How Greed and Violence Are Eroding Our Nation's Character*. New York: St.Martin's.

Ditton, Paul M., and Doris Wilson. 1999. *Truth in Sentencing in State Prisons*. Washington, DC: U.S. Department of Justice.

Downes, David, and Paul Rock. 1982. *Understanding Deviance: A Guide to the Sociology of Crime and Rule Breaking*. Oxford, England: Clarendon.

Durkheim, Émile. [1893] 1964a. *The Division of Labor in Society*. New York: Free Press.

———. [1895] 1964b. *The Rules of Sociological Method*. New York: Free Press.

———. [1897] 1966. *Suicide: A Study in Sociology*. New York: Free Press.

Edelman, Marian Wright. 1992. *The Measure of Our Success: A Letter to My Children and Yours*. Boston: Beacon.

Edsall, Thomas Byrne. 1992. "Willie Horton's Message." *New York Review* (February 13), pp. 7–11.

Elkins, Stanley M. 1968. *Slavery: A Problem in American Institutional and Intellectual Life*. 2d ed. Chicago: University of Chicago Press.

Elliott, Delbert, David Huizinga, and Suzanne Ageton. 1985. *Explaining Delinquency and Drug Use*. Beverly Hills, CA: Sage.

Erikson, Kai T. 1966. *Wayward Puritans: A Study in the Sociology of Deviance*. New York: Wiley.

Esping-Andersen, Gosta. 1990. *The Three Worlds of Welfare Capitalism*. Princeton, NJ: Princeton University Press.

Ewen, Danielle, and Katherine Hart. 2003. *State Budget Cuts Create a Growing Childcare Crisis for Low-Income Working Families*. Washington, DC: Children's Defense Fund.

Farnworth, Margaret, and Michael J. Lieber. 1989. "Strain Theory Revisited: Economic Goals, Educational Means, and Delinquency." *American Sociological Review* 54:263–274.

Featherstone, Richard, and Mathieu Deflem. 2003. "Anomie and Strain: Context and Consequences of Merton's Two Theories." *Sociological Inquiry* 73:471–89.

Federal Bureau of Investigation. Various years. *Crime in the United States*. Washington, DC: U.S. Government Printing Office.

Feeley, Malcolm M., and Jonathan Simon. 1992. "The New Penology: Notes on the Emerging Strategy of Corrections and Its Implications." *Criminology* 30:449–474.

Felson, Marcus. 1998. *Crime & Everyday Life*. 2d ed. Thousand Oaks, CA: Pine Forge Press.

Felson, Richard B., and Steven F. Messner. 1996. "To Kill Or Not to Kill? Lethal Outcomes in Injurious Attacks." *Criminology* 34:519–545.

Fishbein, Diana H. 1990. "Biological Perspectives in Criminology." *Criminology* 28 (February), pp. 27–72.

Flood, Mary, and David Ivanovich. 2004. "Enron's Skilling Charged with Insider Trading." *Houston Chronicle* (February 20). www.houstonchronicle.com.

Fowler, Tom. 2002. "The Pride and the Fall of Enron." *Houston Chronicle* (October 20). www.houstonchronicle.com.

Freeman, Richard B. 1996. "Why Do So Many American Young Men Commit Crimes and What Might We Do about It?" Working paper 5451. Cambridge, MA: National Bureau of Economic Research.

Friedman, Lawrence M. 1993. *Crime and Punishment in American History*. New York: Basic Books.

Friedman, Thomas L. 1996. "Japan Inc. Revisited." *New York Times* (February 25), p. E15.

Gastil, Raymond D. 1971. "Homicide and a Regional Culture of Violence." *American Sociological Review* 36:412–427.

Gibbons, Don C. 1992. *Society, Crime, and Criminal Behavior*. 6th ed. Upper Saddle River, NJ: Prentice Hall.

Gibbs, Nancy. 1999. "Special Report: The Littleton Massacre." *Time* (May 3), pp. 25–36.

Gilliard, Darrell K., and Allen J. Beck. 1997. *Prison and Jail Inmates at Midyear 1996*. Washington, DC: U.S. Department of Justice.

Gilsinan, James F. 1990. *Criminology and Public Policy*. Upper Saddle River, NJ: Prentice Hall.

Gittrich, Greg. 2004. "Crime Saps Spirit of St. Louis." *New York Daily News* (May 31), p. 16.

Golub, Andrew Lang, and Bruce D. Johnson. 1997. "Crack's Decline: Some Surprises Across U.S. Cities." *National Institute of Justice Research in Brief*. Washington, D.C.: Department of Justice .

Gornick, Janet C., and Marcia K. Meyers. 2003. *Families that Work: Policies for Reconciling Parenthood and Employment*. New York: Russell Sage.

Gottfredson, Michael R., and Travis Hirschi. 1990. *A General Theory of Crime*. Stanford, CA: Stanford University Press.

Gouldner, Alvin W. 1970. *The Coming Crisis of Western Sociology*. New York: Basic Books.

Gove, Walter R., Michael Hughes, and Michael Geerken. 1985. "Are Uniform Crime Reports a Valid Indicator of the Index Crimes? An Affirmative Answer with Minor Qualifications." *Criminology* 23:451–501.

Greenhouse, Steven. 2004. "Altering of Worker Time Cards Spurs Growing Number of Suits." *New York Times* (April 4). www.nytimes.com.

Grisolia, James S., Jose Sanmartin, Jose Luis Lujan, and Santiago Grisolia. 1997. *Violence: From Biology to Society*. Amsterdam: Elsevier.

Gurr, Ted Robert. 1989. "Historical Trends in Violent Crime: Europe and the United States." Pp. 21–54 in *Violence in America,* vol. 1: *The History of Crime,* edited by Ted R. Gurr. Newbury Park, CA: Sage.

Gutman, Herbert G. 1976. *The Black Family in Slavery and Freedom, 1750–1925*. New York: Vintage.

Habermas, Jurgen. 1989. "The Crisis of the Welfare State and the Exhaustion of Utopian Energies." Pp. 284–299 in *Jurgen Habermas on Society and Politics: A Reader*, edited by Steven Seidman. Boston: Beacon.

Hacker, Andrew. 1992. *Two Nations: Black and White, Separate, Hostile, Unequal*. New York: Scribner's.

Hackney, Sheldon. 1969. "Southern Violence." Pp. 505–528 in *History of Violence in America: Report of the Task Force on Historical and Comparative Perspectives to the National Commission on the Causes and Prevention of Violence*, edited by Hugh D. Graham and Ted R. Gurr. New York: Bantam.

Hagan, John, John Simpson, and A. R. Gillis. 1987. "Class in the Household: A Power-Control Theory of Gender and Delinquency." *American Journal of Sociology* 92:788–816.

Hancock, Lyn Nell (with Claudia Kalb). 1995. "Returned for Credit." *Newsweek* (May 22), p. 44.

Harcourt, Bernard E. 2001. *Illusion of Order: The False Promise of Broken Windows Policing*. Cambridge, MA: Harvard University Press.

Harris, Marvin. 1981. *America Now: The Anthropology of a Changing Culture*. New York: Simon & Schuster.

Harrison, Bennett, and Barry Bluestone. 1988. *The Great U-Turn: Corporate Restructuring and the Polarizing of America*. New York: Basic Books.

Harrison, Paige M., and Allen J. Beck. 2003. *Prisoners in 2002*. Washington, DC: U.S.Department of Justice.

Harrison, Paige M., and Jennifer C. Karberg. 2003. *Prison and Jail Inmates at Midyear 2002*. Washington, DC: U.S. Department of Justice.

Hawley, F. Frederick, and Steven F. Messner. 1989. "The Southern Violence Construct: A Review of Arguments, Evidence, and the Normative Context." *Justice Quarterly* 6:481–511.

Hearn, Charles R. 1977. *The American Dream in the Great Depression*. Westport, CT: Greenwood.

Heilbroner, Robert. 1991. "A Pivotal Question Unanswered." *The World & I: A Chronicle of Our Changing Era* (November), pp. 538–540.

Hemenway, David. 2004. *Private Guns, Public Health*. Ann Arbor, MI: University of Michigan Press.

Henig, Jeffrey R. 1994. *Rethinking School Choice: Limits of the Market Metaphor*. Princeton, NJ: Princeton University Press.

Hernon, Peter. 1992. "Amid Reality of Nightly Gunfights, Residents Stay Committed to Area." *St. Louis Post-Dispatch* (October 4), pp. 1A, 9A.

Hiaasen, Carl. 1998. "Coke Day Lesson Leaves a Bad Taste." *St. Louis Post-Dispatch* (April 1), p. B7.

Hirschi, Travis. 1969. *Causes of Delinquency*. Berkeley: University of California Press.

———. 1979. "Separate and Unequal Is Better." *Journal of Research in Crime and Delinquency* 16:34–38.

———. 1989. "Exploring Alternatives to Integrated Theory." Pp. 37–49 in *Theoretical Integration in the Study of Deviance and Crime: Problems and Prospects*, edited by Steven F. Messner, Marvin D. Krohn, and Allen E. Liska. Albany: State University of New York Press.

Hobbes, Thomas. [1651] 1958. *Leviathan*. Indianapolis, IN: Bobbs-Merrill.

Hochschild, Arlie. 1989. *The Second Shift*. New York: Avon Books.

Hochschild, Jennifer. 1995. *Facing Up to the American Dream: Race, Class, and the Soul of the Nation*. Princeton, NJ: Princeton University Press.

Hodgins, Sheilagh. 1992. "Mental Disorder, Intellectual Deficiency, and Crime." *Archives of General Psychiatry* 49:476–483.

Ince, Adamma. 2003. "Double Dutch in a War Zone." *Village Voice* (November 26 – December 2). http://www.villagevoice.com/print/issues/0348/ince.php.

Interpol. 1996–1997. *International Crime Statistics*. Saint Cloud, France: International Criminal Police Organization.

Jacobs, Bruce A. 1999. *Dealing Crack: The Social World of Streetcorner Selling*. Boston: Northeastern University Press.

Johnson, Allan G. 1991. *The Forest for the Trees: An Introduction to Sociological Thinking*. San Diego, CA: Harcourt Brace Jovanovich.

Johnson, Byron R., Spencer De Li, David B. Larson, and Michael McCullough. 2000. "A Systematic Review of the Religiosity and Delinquency Literature." *Journal of Contemporary Criminal Justice* 16:32–52.

Johnson, Carrie. 2004. "Founder of Enron Pleads Not Guilty." *Washington Post* (July 9), pp. A1, A12.

Kappeler, Victor E. Mark Blumberg, and Gary W. Potter. 1993. *The Mythology of Crime and Criminal Justice*. Prospect Heights, IL: Waveland.

Keillor, Garrison. 1992. "Enjoy." *New York Times* (July 13), p. A15.

Kincaid, Cliff. 2003. "Crime in Iraq Vs. Washington DC." *Media Monitor* (September 12). http://www.aim.org/publications/media_monitor/2003/09/12.html.

Klaus, Patsy. 1994. *The Costs of Crime to Victims*. Washington, DC: U.S. Department of Justice.

Kleck, Gary. 1991. *Point Blank: Guns and Violence in America*. New York: Aldine de Gruyter.

Kleck, Gary, and Karen McElrath. 1991. "The Effects of Weaponry on Human Violence." *Social Forces* 69:11–21.

Klein, Joe. 1992. "Copping a Domestic Agenda." *Newsweek* (December 7), p. 29.

Koretz, Gene. 2003. "Land of Opportunity." *Business Week* (June 30), Issue 3839.

Kornhauser, Ruth R. 1978. *Social Sources of Delinquency: An Appraisal of Analytic Models*. Chicago: University of Chicago Press.

Kozol, Jonathan. 1991. *Savage Inequalities: Children in America's Schools*. New York: Crown.

———. 1992. "Whittle and the Privateers." *The Nation* (September 21), pp. 272–278.

Kroeber, A. L., and Talcott Parsons. 1958. "The Concepts of Culture and of Social System." *American Sociological Review* 23:582–583.

LaFree, Gary. 1998. *Losing Legitimacy: Street Crime and the Decline of Social Institutions in America*. Boulder, CO: Westview.

———. 1999. "A Summary and Review of Cross-National Comparative Studies of Homicide." Pp. 125–145 in *Homicide: A Sourcebook of Social Research*, edited by M. Dwayne Smith and Margaret A. Zahn. Thousand Oaks, CA: Sage.

Lane, Ann J., ed. 1971. *The Debate over Slavery: Stanley Elkins and His Critics*. Urbana: University of Illinois Press.

Langan, Patrick A., and David J. Levin. 2002. *Recidivism of Prisoners Released in 1994.* Washington, DC: U.S. Department of Justice.

Lasch, Christopher. 1977. *Haven in a Heartless World: The Family Besieged.* New York: Basic Books.

Levitan, Sar A., Richard S. Belous, and Frank Gallo. 1988. *What's Happening to the American Family?* Baltimore: Johns Hopkins University Press.

Levy, Frank. 1988. *Dollars and Dreams.* New York: Norton.

Lewin, Tamar. 2000. "Leaders from Other Professions Reshape America's Schools, from Top to Bottom." *New York Times* (June 8) (http://www.nytimes.com/library/national/060800nat-schools-edu.html).

Lewis, Oscar. 1966. "The Culture of Poverty." *Scientific American* 215:19–25.

Lilly, J. Robert, Francis T. Cullen, and Richard A. Ball. 1989. *Criminological Theory: Context and Consequences.* Newbury Park, CA: Sage.

Liska, Allen E. 1987. *Perspectives on Deviance.* 2d ed. Upper Saddle River, NJ: Prentice Hall.

Liska, Allen E., and Steven F. Messner. 1999. *Perspectives on Crime and Deviance.* 3d ed. Upper Saddle River, NJ: Prentice Hall.

Little, Joan. 1992. "Pupils Told to 'Run for Your Lives." *St. Louis Post-Dispatch* (February 22), pp. 1A, 8A.

Long, Elizabeth. 1985. *The American Dream and the Popular Novel.* Boston: Routledge & Kegan Paul.

Lynch, James. 1995. "Crime in International Perspective." Pp. 11–38 in *Crime,* edited by James Q. Wilson and Joan PetersiliaWilson. San Francisco: ICS.

MacLeod, Jay. 1987. *Ain't No Makin' It: Leveled Aspirations in a Low-Income Neighborhood.* Boulder, CO: Westview.

Mansnerus, Laura. 1993. "Kids of the 90's: A Bolder Breed." *New York Times* (April 4), sec. 4A , pp. 14–15.

Marriott, Michel. 1995. "Living in 'Lockdown.' *Newsweek* (January 23), pp. 56–57.

Marx, Karl, and Frederick Engels. 1968. *Selected Works.* New York: International Publishers.

Mascaro, Lisa. 2004. "Gangs Deadlier Than Terror." *Los Angeles Daily News* (January 11). www.dailynews.com.

Massey, Douglas S., and Nancy Denton. 1993. *American Apartheid: Segregation and the Making of the Underclass.* Cambridge, MA: Harvard University Press.

Mauer, Marc. 1999. *Race to Incarcerate.* New York: New Press.

———. 2003. *Comparative International Rates of Incarceration: An Examination of Causes and Trends.* Washington, DC: Sentencing Project.

Mayhew, Pat. 1993. "American Crime Rates Not Highest." *Overcrowded Times* 4:1, 8–11.

McPhee, Michele, Alice McQuillan, and Dave Goldiner. 2004. "Dueling View of Roof Shoot." *New York Daily News: The Front Page.* Available online at http://www.nydailynews.com/front/story/158409p-139017c.html.

Menard, Scott. 1995. "A Developmental Test of Mertonian Anomie Theory." *Journal of Research in Crime and Delinquency* 32:136–174.

Merton, Robert K. 1938. "Social Structure and Anomie." *American Sociological Review* 3:672–682.

————. 1959. "Social Conformity, Deviation, and Opportunity Structures: A Comment on the Contributions of Dubin and Cloward." *American Sociological Review* 24:177–189.

————. 1964. "Anomie, Anomia, and Social Interaction." Pp. 213–242 in *Anomie and Deviant Behavior*, edited by Marshall Clinard. New York: Free Press.

————. 1968. *Social Theory and Social Structure*. New York: Free Press.

Messner, Steven F. 1988. "Merton's 'Social Structure and Anomie': The Road Not Taken." *Deviant Behavior* 9:33–53.

————. 2003. "Understanding Cross-National Variation in Criminal Violence." Pp. 701–716 in *Handbook of Research on Violence*, edited by W. Heitmeyer and J. Hagan. Dordrecht, The Netherlands: Kluwer Academic Publishers.

————. 2004. "An Institutional-Anomie Theory of Crime: Continuities and Elaborations in the Study of Social Structure and Anomie." *Cologne Journal of Sociology and Social Psychology* 43:93–109.

Messner, Steven F., and Reid M. Golden. 1992. "Racial Inequality and Racially Disaggregated Crime Rates: An Assessment of Alternative Theoretical Explanations." *Criminology* 30:421–445.

Messner, Steven F., and Richard Rosenfeld. 1997. "Political Restraint of the Market and Levels of Criminal Homicide: A Cross-National Application of Institutional-Anomie Theory." *Social Forces* 75:1393–1416.

————. 2004. "Institutionalizing Criminological Theory." Pp. 83–105 in *Beyond Empiricism: Institutions and Intentions in the Study of Crime. Advances in Criminological Theory*, Vol. 13, edited by Joan McCord. Piscataway, NJ: Transaction Books.

Messner, Steven F., and Robert J. Sampson. 1991. "The Sex Ratio, Family Disruption, and Rates of Violent Crime: The Paradox of Demographic Structure." *Social Forces* 69:693–713.

MicroCase Corporation. 1999–2000. *MicroCase Data Archive*. Bellevue, WA: MicroCase Corporation.

Miller, Walter B. 1958. "Lower Class Culture as a Generating Milieu of Gang Delinquency." *Journal of Social Issues* 14:5–19.

Mills, C. Wright. 1943. "The Professional Ideology of Social Pathologists." *American Journal of Sociology* 49:165–180.

Murray, David W. 1994. "Poor Suffering Bastards." *Policy Review* (Spring) 9–15.

Neapolitan, Jerome L. 1997. *Cross-National Crime: A Research Review and Sourcebook*. Westport, CT: Greenwood Press.

Nevins, Allan. 1968. *James Truslow Adams: Historian of the American Dream*. Urbana: University of Illinois Press.

New York Times. 1990. "Stunning Justice in the Milken Case." (November 22), p. A26.

————. 1992. "A Downgraded Detroit Cries Foul." (November 3), pp. C1, C4.

————. 1994. "Clinton Urges Quick Passage for Crime Bill." (June 6), p. A9.

————. 1998. *The New York Times Almanac 1999*. New York: Penguin.

————. 2000. "New Jersey's Excessive Senate Race." (June 8) http://www.nytimes.com/060800/editorial/08thu3.html.

Newman, Graeme, and Gregory J. Howard. 1999. "Introduction: Data Sources and Their Use." Pp. 1–23 in *Global Report on Crime and Justice*, edited by Graeme Newman. New York: Oxford University Press.

Newsweek. 1992. "U.S.Troops: Black like Me." (December 21), p. 29.

———. 1999. "Anatomy of a Massacre." (May 3), pp. 25–31.

Nightingale, Carl Husemoller. 1993. *On the Edge: A History of Poor Black Children and Their American Dreams*. New York: Basic Books.

Nisbet, Robert. 1971. "The Study of Social Problems." Pp. 1–25 in *Contemporary Social Problems*, 3d ed., edited by Robert K. Merton and Robert Nisbet. New York: Harcourt Brace Jovanovich.

O'Brien, Robert M. 1985. *Crime and Victimization Data*. Beverly Hills, CA: Sage.

O'Connor, John J. 1993. "TV Likes to Explore Violence That May Inspire." *New York Times* (December 9), p. B3.

O'Keefe, Bryan. 2003. "Use Your Head to Be Brains Behind Billboard." *Albany Times Union* (December 11), p. A2.

Orru, Marco. 1987. *Anomie: History and Meanings*. Boston: Allen & Unwin.

———. 1990. "Merton's Instrumental Theory of Anomie." Pp. 231–240 in Robert K. Merton *Consensus and Controversy*, edited by Jon Clark, Celia Modgil, and Sohan Modgil. London: Falmer.

Parascandola, Rocco, and Luis Perez. 2004. "Innocent Victim: 'No Justification' for Killing by Cop." *Newsday* (January 25), Queens Edition, p. A3.

Park, Robert E., Ernest W. Burgess, and Roderick D. McKenzie. [1925] 1967. *The City*. Chicago: University of Chicago Press.

Parsons, Talcott. 1951. *The Social System*. New York: Free Press.

———. 1964. *Essays in Sociological Theory*. Rev. ed. New York: Free Press.

Passas, Nikos. 1990. "Anomie and Corporate Deviance." *Contemporary Crises* 14:157–178.

———. 1997. "Anomie, Reference Groups, and Relative Deprivation." Pp. 62–94 in *The Future of Anomie Theory*, edited by Nikos Passas and Robert Agnew. Boston: Northeastern University Press.

Passas, Nikos, and Robert Agnew. 1997. *The Future of Anomie Theory*. Boston: Northeastern University Press.

Patterson, Orlando. 1999. "When 'They' Are 'Us.' " *New York Times* (April 30), p. A31.

Petersilia, Joan. 1999. "Parole and Prisoner Reentry in the United States." Pp. 479–529 in *Prisons*, edited by M. Tonry and J. Petersilia. Chicago: University of Chicago Press.

Pfohl, Stephen J. 1985. *Images of Deviance and Social Control: A Sociological History*. New York: McGraw-Hill.

Philadelphia Inquirer. 2004. "Brand-Name Field Trips A Total Sellout." (May 27), p. 26.

Polanyi, Karl. [1944] 1957. *The Great Transformation: The Political and Economic Origins of Our Time*. Boston: Beacon.

Potter, Gary W., and Victor E. Kappeler, eds. *Constructing Crime: Perspectives on Making News and Social Problems*. Prospect Heights, IL: Waveland.

Press, Eyal, and Jennifer Washburn. 2000. *The Atlantic Monthly* (Digital Edition) (March 2000). http://www.theatlantic.com/issues/2000/03/press.htm.

Presser, Harriet. 2003. *Working in a 24/7 Economy: Challenges for American Families*. New York: Russell Sage.

Quindlen, Anna. 2004. "An Apology to the Graduates." *Newsweek* (May 17), p. 70.

Raine, Adrian. 2002. "The Biological Basis of Crime." Pp. 43–74 in *Crime: Public Policies for Crime Control* edited by J. Q. Wilson and J. Petersilia. Oakland, CA: ICS Press.

Rainwater, Lee. 1974. *What Money Buys: Inequality and the Social Meanings of Income.* New York: Basic Books.

Reichel, Philip L. 2002. *Comparative Criminal Justice Systems.* 3rd ed. Upper Saddle River, NJ: Prentice Hall.

Reiss, Albert J., Jr., and Jeffrey A. Roth, eds. 1993. *Understanding and Preventing Violence.* Washington, DC: National Academy Press.

Reuter, Peter. 1984. "Social Control in Illegal Markets." Pp. 29–58 in *Toward a General of Theory of Social Control*, vol. 2, edited by Donald Black. New York: Academic Press.

Richardson, Lynda. 1992. "Somalia? In the South Bronx, They Ask, Why Not Aid Us?" *New York Times* (December 14), p. A8.

Riedel, Marc. 1999. "Sources of Homicide Data: A Review and Comparison." Pp. 75–95 in *Homicide: A Sourcebook of Social Research*, edited by M. Dwayne Smith and Margaret A. Zahn. Thousand Oaks, CA: Sage.

Ropers, Richard H. 1991. *Persistent Poverty: The American Dream Turned Nightmare.* New York: Plenum.

Rose, Dina R., and Todd R. Clear. 1998. "Incarceration, Social Capital, and Crime: Implications for Social Disorganization Theory." *Criminology* 36:441–479.

Rosenberg, Mark L., and James A. Mercy. 1986. "Homicide: Epidemiologic Analysis at the National Level." *Bulletin of the New York Academy of Medicine* 62:376–399.

Rosenfeld, Richard. 1989. "Robert Merton's Contributions to the Sociology of Deviance." *Sociological Inquiry* 59:453–466.

———. 2004a. "Terrorism and Criminology." Pp. 19–32 in *Terrorism and Counter-Terrorism: Criminological Perspectives*, edited by Mathieu Deflem. London: Elsevier.

———. 2004b. "The Case of the Unsolved Crime Decline." *Scientific American* (February), pp. 82–89.

Rosenfeld, Richard, and Kimberly F. Kempf. 1991. "The Scope and Purposes of Corrections: Exploring Alternative Responses to Crowding." *Crime and Delinquency* 37:481–505.

Rosenfeld, Richard, Joel Wallman, and Robert Fornango. 2005. "The Contribution of Ex-Prisoners to Crime Rates." Pp. 80–104 in *Prisoner Reentry and Public Safety*, edited by Jeremy Travis and Christy Visher. New York: Cambridge.

Rosoff, Stephen M., Henry N. Pontell, and Robert H. Tillman. 2003. *Looting America: Greed, Corruption, Villains, and Victims.* Upper Saddle River, NJ: Prentice Hall.

Rossi, Peter H., Emily Waite, Christine E. Bose, and Richard E. Berk. 1974. "The Seriousness of Crimes: Normative Structure and Individual Differences." *American Sociological Review* 39:224–237.

Sampson, Robert J. 1987. "Urban Black Violence: The Effect of Male Joblessness and Family Disruption." *American Journal of Sociology* 93:348–382.

Sampson, Robert J., and W. Byron Groves. 1989. "Community Structure and Crime: Testing Social-Disorganization Theory." *American Journal of Sociology* 94:774–802.

Sampson, Robert J., Jeffrey D. Morenoff, and Thomas Gannon-Rowley. 2002. "Assessing 'Neighborhood Effects': Social Processes and New Directions in Research." *Annual Review of Sociology* 28:443–478.

Sampson, Robert J., Stephen W. Raudenbush, and Felton Earls. 1997. "Neighborhoods and Violent Crime: A Multilevel Study of Collective Efficacy." *Science* 277: 918–924.

Samuelson, Paul A., and William D. Nordhaus. 1989. *Macroeconomics: A Version of Economics*. 13th ed. New York: McGraw-Hill.

Samuelson, Robert J. 1992. "How Our American Dream Unraveled." *Newsweek* (March 2), pp. 32–39.

Sanger, David E. 1993. "After Gunman's Acquittal, Japan Struggles to Understand America." *New York Times* (May 25), pp. A1, A7.

———. 1994. "2 Students' Killings in California Confirm Fear of America in Japan." *New York Times* (March 29), pp.A1, A10 .

Schur, Edwin M. 1969. *Our Criminal Society: The Social and Legal Sources of Crime in America*. Upper Saddle River, NJ: Prentice Hall.

Schwartz, Barry. 1994a. "On Morals and Markets." *Criminal Justice Ethics* 13:61–69.

———. 1994b. *The Costs of Living: How Market Freedom Erodes the Best Things in Life*. New York: Norton.

Schwartz, Delmore. [1937] 1978. *In Dreams Begin Responsibilities and Other Stories*. New York: New Directions.

Sellin, Thorsten, and Marvin Wolfgang. 1964. *The Measurement of Delinquency*. New York: Wiley.

Shaw, Clifford R., and Henry D. McKay. 1969. *Juvenile Delinquency in Urban Areas*. Rev. ed. Chicago: University of Chicago Press.

Sheley, Joseph F., and James D. Wright. 1995. *In the Line of Fire: Youth, Guns, and Violence in Urban America*. New York: Aldine.

Shelley, Louise I. 1981. *Crime and Modernization: The Impact of Industrialization and Urbanization on Crime*. Carbondale: Southern Illinois University Press.

Short, James F., Jr. 1985. "The Level of Explanation Problem in Criminology." Pp. 51–72 in *Theoretical Methods in Criminology*, edited by Robert F. Meier. Beverly Hills, CA: Sage.

Sidel, Ruth. 1986. *Women and Children Last: The Plight of Poor Women in Affluent America*. New York: Penguin Books.

Skogan, Wesley G. 1990. *Disorder and Decline: Crime and the Spiral of Decay in American Neighborhoods*. Berkeley: University of California Press.

Snyder, James, and Gerald Patterson. 1987. "Family Interaction and Delinquent Behavior." Pp. 216–243 in *Handbook of Juvenile Delinquency*, edited by Herbert C. Quay. New York: Wiley.

Soll, Rick. 1993. "The Killing Fields." *Chicago* (March), pp. 54–59, 97–99.

South, Scott J., and Katherine Trent. 1988. "Sex Ratios and Women's Roles: A Cross-National Analysis." *American Journal of Sociology* 93:1096–1115.

Spelman, William. 2000. "The Limited Importance of Prison Expansion." In *The Crime Drop in America*, edited by Alfred Blumstein and Joel Wallman. New York: Cambridge University Press.

St. Louis Post-Dispatch. 2000. "Clinton Bars Bias against US Employees with Kids." (May 3), p. A12.

Staples, Brent. 1993. "Confronting Slaughter in the Streets." *New York Times* (November 5), p. A12.

Staples, Robert. 1987. *The Urban Plantation: Racism and Colonialism in the Post Civil Rights Era*. Oakland, CA: Black Scholar Press.

Stark, Rodney. 1987. "Deviant Paces: A Theory of the Ecology of Crime." *Criminology* 25:893–909.

Steffensmeier, Darrell, and Emilie Allan. 1995. "Criminal Behavior: Gender and Age." Pp. 83–113 in *Criminology*, edited by Joseph F. Sheley. Belmont, CA: Wadsworth.

Steinberg, Stephen. 1981. *The Ethnic Myth: Race, Ethnicity, and Class in America*. New York: Atheneum.

Stitt, B. Grant, and David J. Giacopassi. 1992. "Trends in the Connectivity of Theory and Research in Criminology." *The Criminologist* 17:1, 3–6.

Strosnider, Kim. 1997. "A Public-College President Focuses on Raising Funds from Private Sources." *The Chronicle of Higher Education* (March 14), pp. A31, A33.

Sullivan, Mercer L. 1988. *"Getting Paid": Youth Crime and Work in the Inner City*. Ithaca, NY: Cornell University Press.

Sullivan, Ronald. 1992. "Milken's Sentence Reduced by Judge; 7 Months Are Left." *New York Times* (August 6), pp. A1, D17.

Surette, Ray. 1992. *Media, Crime, and Criminal Justice: Images and Realities*. Pacific Grove, CA: Brooks/Cole.

Sutherland, Edwin H. 1947. *Principles of Criminology*. Philadelphia: Lippincott.

———. 1949. *White Collar Crime*. New York: Holt, Rinehart & Winston.

Sutton, John R. 2004. "The Political Economy of Imprisonment in Affluent Western Democracies, 1960–1990." *American Sociological Review* 69:170–189.

Sykes, Gresham M., and Francis T. Cullen. 1992. *Criminology*. 2d ed. New York: Harcourt Brace Jovanovich.

Taylor, Charles Lewis, and David A. Jodice. 1983. *World Handbook of Political and Social Indicators*. 3d ed. Vol. 1 *Cross-National Attributes and Rates of Change*. New Haven, CT: Yale University Press.

Taylor, Ian, Paul Walton, and Jock Young. 1973. *The New Criminology: For a Social Theory of Deviance*. New York: Harper & Row.

The Teaching Professor. 1994. "The Customer-Driven" Classroom: A Rebuttal." (November 8), pp. 1–2.

Teles, Steven M., and Mark Kleiman. 2000. "Escape From America's Prison Policy." *American Prospect* (September 11), pp. 30–34.

Terry, Don. 1992. "Where Even a Grade School Is No Refuge from Gunfire." *New York Times* (October 17), pp. A1, A6.

Tetzeli, Rick. 1992. "Most Dangerous and Endangered." *Fortune* (August 10), pp. 78–81.

Thomas, Charles W. 1987. *Corrections in America: Problems of the Past and the Present*. Newbury Park, CA: Sage.

Thompson, Linda, and Alexis J. Walker. 1991. "Gender in Families: Women and Men in Marriage, Work, and Parenthood." Pp. 76–102 in *Contemporary Families: Looking Forward, Looking Back*, edited by Alan Booth. Minneapolis, MN: National Council on Family Relations.

Thomson, Susan C. 1992. "Job Oriented Courses Fuel Boom in Students at Private Colleges." *St. Louis Post-Dispatch* (December 8), p. 3A.

Time Daily. 2000. "A Murder Case Puts Police Methods on Trial." (January 31). (http://www.time.com/time/daily/0,2960,38484,00.html).

Time Magazine. 2000. "Black and Blue." (March 6). (http://www.time.com/ti. . .zine/articles/0,3266,39946,00.html).

Tittle, Charles R. 1995. *Control Balance: Toward a General Theory of Deviance.* Boulder, CO: Westview.

Tolson, Mike. 2004. "For Skilling, Failure Never an Option." *Houston Chronicle* (February 19). www.houstonchronicle.com .

Tonry, Michael. 1995. *Malign Neglect: Race, Crime, and Punishment in America.* New York: Oxford.

Travis, Jeremy. 2001. "But They All Come Back: Rethinking Prisoner Reentry." *Corrections Management Quarterly* 5:23–33.

Travis, Jeremy, Amy L. Solomon, and Michelle Waul. 2001. *From Prison to Home: The Dimensions and Consequences of Prisoner Reentry.* Washington, DC: Urban Institute.

Truell, Peter. 1995. "Milken, Barred as Financier, Puts His Stamp on Big Deals." *New York Times* (October 1), pp. 1, 20.

Turk, Austin T. 1969. *Criminality and Legal Order.* Chicago: Rand-McNally.

Turner, Jonathan H. 1978. *The Structure of Sociological Theory.* Rev. ed. Homewood, IL: Dorsey.

Turner, Jonathan H., and David Musick. 1985. *American Dilemmas: A Sociological Interpretation of Enduring Social Issues.* New York: Columbia University Press.

USA Today. 2002. "Time to Revisit the Costly Policy of Locking Up Drug Offenders." (September 30).

U.S. Bureau of the Census. 1998. *Marital Status and Living Arrangements: March 1996.* Current Population Reports, P20–496. Washington, DC: U.S. Department of Commerce.

———. 2003. *Statistical Abstract of the United States: 2002.* http://www.census.gov/prod/www/statistical-abstract-02.html.

———. 2004. *Historical Income Tables.* Washington, DC. http://www.census.gov/hhes/income/histinc/f02.html.

U.S. Congress House Committee on Government Operations. 1988. *Combatting Fraud, Abuse, and Misconduct in the Nation's Financial Institutions: Current Federal Efforts Are Inadequate,* Rept. 100–1088 and Errata. Washington, DC: U.S. Government Printing Office.

Valdmanis, Thor. 2003. "Illegal Trading Appears Rampant." *USA Today* (September 12). www.usatoday.com.

van den Haag, Ernest. 1978. "No Excuse for Crime." Pp. 205–211 in *Crime in Society,* edited by Leonard D. Savitz and Norman Johnston. New York: Wiley.

van Dijk, Jan, and Kristiina Kangaspunta. 2000. "Piecing Together the Cross-National Crime Puzzle." *National Institute of Justice Journal* (January), pp. 34–41.

Vaughn, Diane. 1983. *Controlling Unlawful Organizational Behavior: Social Structure and Corporate Misconduct.* Chicago: University of Chicago Press.

Vold, George B., and Thomas J. Bernard. 1986. *Theoretical Criminology.* 3d ed. New York: Oxford University Press.

Vold, George B., Thomas J. Bernard, and Jeffrey B. Snipes. 2002. *Theoretical Criminology,* 5th ed. New York: Oxford University Press.

Volland, Victor. 1994. "School Program Rewards High Grades." *St. Louis Post-Dispatch* (March 10), pp. 1–2B.

Waldman, Steven, and Karen Springen. 1992. "Too Old, Too Fast?" *Newsweek* (November 16), pp. 80–88.

Walker, Samuel. 1989. *Sense and Nonsense about Crime: A Policy Guide.* 2d ed. Pacific Grove, CA: Brooks/Cole.

Walters, Glenn D. 1992. "A Meta-Analysis of the Gene-Crime Relationship." *Criminology* 30:595–613.

White House News Release. 2004. "President Discusses America's Leadership in Global War on Terror" (January 22). www.whitehouse.gov/news/releases/2004/01/.

Wicker, Tom. 1991. *One of Us: Richard Nixon and the American Dream.* New York: Random House.

Wilkerson, Isabel. 1992. "27 Years Later, the Young Clearly Hear Malcolm X." *New York Times* (November 18), pp. A1, B7.

Will, George. 1992. "Democrats Can Win If They Remember What Reagan Said." *Albany Times Union* (July 12), p. E5.

———. 2004. "A Cop on the Beat in Gangland L. A." *Albany Times Union* (March 21), p. B5.

Wills, Gary. 2000. "Gun Abundance Causes Fear." *Albany Times Union* (March 25), p. A7.

Wilson, James Q. 1975. *Thinking about Crime.* New York: Basic Books.

Wilson, James Q., and Richard J. Herrnstein. 1985. *Crime and Human Nature.* New York: Simon & Schuster.

Wilson, William Julius. 1987. *The Truly Disadvantaged: The Inner City, the Underclass, and Public Policy.* Chicago: University of Chicago Press.

———. 1996. *When Work Disappears: The World of the New Urban Poor.* New York: Knopf.

Wolfe, Alan. 1989. *Whose Keeper? Social Science and Moral Obligation.* Berkeley: University of California Press.

Wolff, Edward N. 1995. "How the Pie is Sliced: America's Growing Concentration of Wealth." *The American Prospect* (Summer), pp. 58–64.

Wolfgang, Marvin E., and Franco Ferracuti. 1967. *The Subculture of Violence.* London: Tavistock.

Wolfgang, Marvin E., Robert M. Figlio, Paul E. Tracy, and Simon I. Singer. 1985. *The National Survey of Crime Severity.* Washington, DC: U.S. Government Printing Office.

Wood, Daniel B. 2004. "As Gangs Rise, So Do Calls for US-Wide Dragnet." *Christian Science Monitor* (February 4). www.csmonitor.com.

World Health Organization. 1995. *World Health Statistics Annual.* Geneva: World Health Organization.

———. 1996. *World Health Statistics Annual.* Geneva: World Health Organization.

Wright, Charles, and R. E. Hilbert. 1980. "Value Implications of the Functional Theory of Deviance." *Social Problems* 28:205–219.

Zahn, Margaret A. 1989. "Homicide in the Twentieth Century: Trends, Types, and Causes." Pp. 216–234 in *Violence in America, vol. 1: The History of Crime,* edited by Ted R. Gurr. Newbury Park, CA: Sage.

Zimring, Franklin E. 2001. "Imprisonment Rates and the New Politics of Criminal Punishment." Pp. 145–149 in *Mass Imprisonment: Social Causes and Consequences*, edited by D. Garland. London: Sage.

Zimring, Franklin E., and Gordon Hawkins. 1997. *Crime Is Not the Problem: Lethal Violence in America*. New York: Oxford University Press.

Index